2012 Conference of the North American Chapter of the Association for Computational Linguistics: Human Language Technologies (NAACL HLT 2012)

Student Research Workshop

Montreal, Quebec, Canada
4 June 2012

ISBN: 978-1-62276-233-0

Printed from e-media with permission by:

Curran Associates, Inc.
57 Morehouse Lane
Red Hook, NY 12571

Some format issues inherent in the e-media version may also appear in this print version.

Printed by Curran Associates, Inc. (2012)

Association for Computational Linguistics
209 N. Eighth Street
Stroudsburg, Pennsylvania 18360

Phone: 1-570-476-8006
Fax: 1-570-476-0860

acl@aclweb.org

Additional copies of this publication are available from:

Curran Associates, Inc.
57 Morehouse Lane
Red Hook, NY 12571 USA
Phone: 845-758-0400
Fax: 845-758-2634
Email: curran@proceedings.com
Web: www.proceedings.com

Introduction

Welcome to the NAACL Student Research Workshop. This year, papers were submitted to two separate tracks: Research Paper and Thesis Proposal. We received 18 submissions from ten countries and accepted 12. Of the accepted papers, seven were research papers and five were thesis proposals. Each accepted paper will be presented as a poster during the NAACL-HLT 2012 Poster Session and assigned an experienced mentor who will provide constructive feedback.

The workshop received many excellent submissions this year, and we thank our Program Committee for their thoughtful reviews. We would also like to thank the entire NAACL-HLT 2012 Organizing Committee, especially Jennifer Chu-Carroll, Eric Fossler-Lussier, Priscilla Rasmussen, Smaranda Muresan, and Dirk Hovy. We are also grateful to our faculty advisors, Roger Levy and Ani Nenkova, for their guidance and involvement. Our warmest gratitude goes to the individuals who agreed to contribute their time and expertise and serve as mentors for this workshop. Finally, we would like to acknowledge the generous support of the U.S. National Science Foundation (Award Number IIS-1220521), which made it possible for us to offer most of the presenters conference registration, accommodation, and travel support.

Program Committee:

Delphine Bernhard, University of Strasbourg
Steven Bethard, University of Colorado Boulder
Klinton Bicknell, University of California San Diego
Phil Blunsom, Oxford University
Ben Carterette, University of Delaware
Berthold Crysmann, CNRS & Université Paris-Diderot
Hal Daumè III, University of Maryland
Seniz Demir, Tubitak
Mark Dredze, Johns Hopkins University
Jacob Eisenstein, Georgia Tech
Micha Elsner, University of Edinburg
Amit Goyal, University of Maryland
Ben Hachey, Macquarie University
Matt Huenerfauth, City University of New York
Kevin Knight, University of Southern California
Zornitsa Kozareva, University of Southern California
Udo Kruschwitz, University of Essex
Tom Kwiatkowski, University of Edinburgh
Maider Lehr, Oregon Health and Science University
Diane Litman, University of Pittsburgh
Yang Liu, University of Texas at Dallas
Adam Lopez, Johns Hopkins University
Bin Lu, City University of Hong Kong
Prashanth Mannem, Indian Institute of Technology Hyderabad
Sameer Maskey, Columbia University
Taniya Mishra, AT&T
Jeremy Nicholson, University of Melbourne
Joakim Nivre, Uppsala University
Brendan O'Connor, Carnegie Mellon University
Martha Palmer, University of Colorado Boulder
Pavel Pecina, Charles University in Prague
Brian Pluss, The Open University
Hamid R. Chinaei, Laval University
Sujith Ravi, Yahoo! Research
Carolyn Penstein Rosè, Carnegie Mellon University
Andrew Rosenberg, City University of New York
Nathan Schneider, Carnegie Mellon University
Sabine Schulte im Walde, University of Stuttgart
Elizabeth Shriberg, Microsoft Speech Labs
Svetlana Stoyanchev, Columbia University
Joel Tetreault, Educational Testing Service

Lu Wang, Cornell University
Arthur Ward, University of Pittsburgh
Bonnie Webber, University of Edinburgh
Yorick Wilks, University of Sheffield
Sandra Williams, The Open University
Ainur Yessenalina, Cornell University

Student Co-Chairs:

Rivka Levitan, Columbia University
Myle Ott, Cornell University

Faculty Advisors:

Roger Levy, University of California San Diego
Ani Nenkova, University of Pennsylvania

Table of Contents

Conference Program

Monday, June 4, 2012

(6:00-9:00) Research Papers

Finding the Right Supervisor: Expert-Finding in a University Domain
Fawaz Alarfaj, Udo Kruschwitz, David Hunter and Chris Fox

Automatic Animacy Classification
Samuel R. Bowman and Harshit Chopra

Beauty Before Age? Applying Subjectivity to Automatic English Adjective Ordering
Felix Hill

Indexing Google 1T for low-turnaround wildcarded frequency queries
Steinar Vittersø Kaldager

Unified Extraction of Health Condition Descriptions
Ivelina Nikolova

Choosing an Evaluation Metric for Parser Design
Woodley Packard

Domain-Specific Semantic Relatedness From Wikipedia: Can A Course Be Transferred?
Beibei Yang and Jesse M. Heines

(6:00-9:00) Thesis Proposals

Using Ontology-based Approaches to Representing Speech Transcripts for Automated Speech Scoring
Miao Chen

Deep Unsupervised Feature Learning for Natural Language Processing
Stephan Gouws

Automatic Metrics for Genre-specific Text Quality
Annie Louis

Finding the Right Supervisor: Expert-Finding in a University Domain

Fawaz Alarfaj, Udo Kruschwitz, David Hunter and Chris Fox
School of Computer Science and Electronic Engineering
University of Essex
Colchester, CO4 3SQ, UK
{falarf, udo, dkhunter, foxcj}@essex.ac.uk

Abstract

Effective knowledge management is a key factor in the development and success of any organisation. Many different methods have been devised to address this need. Applying these methods to identify the experts within an organisation has attracted a lot of attention. We look at one such problem that arises within universities on a daily basis but has attracted little attention in the literature, namely the problem of a searcher who is trying to identify a potential PhD supervisor, or, from the perspective of the university's research office, to allocate a PhD application to a suitable supervisor. We reduce this problem to identifying a ranked list of experts for a given query (representing a research area).

We report on experiments to find experts in a university domain using two different methods to extract a ranked list of candidates: a database-driven method and a data-driven method. The first one is based on a fixed list of experts (e.g. all members of academic staff) while the second method is based on automatic Named-Entity Recognition (NER). We use a graded weighting based on proximity between query and candidate name to rank the list of candidates. As a baseline, we use a system that ranks candidates simply based on frequency of occurrence within the top documents.

1 Introduction

The knowledge and expertise of individuals are significant resources for organisation. Managing this intangible resource effectively and efficiently constitutes an essential and very important task (Nonaka and Takeuchi, 1995; Law and Ngai, 2008). Approaching experts is the primary and most direct way of utilising their knowledge (Yang and Huh, 2008; Li et al., 2011). Therefore, it is important to have a means of locating the right experts within organisations. The expert-finding task can be categorised as an information retrieval task similar to a web search, but where the results are people rather than documents. An expert-finding system allows users to input a query, and it returns a ranked list of experts.

Here we look at a university context. We start with a real-world problem which is to identify a list of experts within an academic environment, e.g. a university intranet. The research reported here is based on an empirical study of a simple but effective method in which a system that applies the concept of expert-finding has been designed and implemented. The proposed system will contribute to provide an expert-search service to all of the university's stakeholders.

Expert-finding systems require two main resources in order to function: a list of candidates and a collection of data from which the evidence of expertise can be extracted. We present two approaches to address this problem, a database-driven and a data-driven method using NER. The main difference between the two methods is the way in which the candidates' list is constructed. In the database method, the candidates are simply selected from a known list of experts, e.g. the university's academic staff. In the NER method, the candidates are extracted *automatically* from the pages returned by an

Proceedings of the NAACL HLT 2012 Student Research Workshop, pages 1–6,
Montréal, Canada, June 3-8, 2012.

underlying search engine. This method promises to be more useful for finding experts from a wider (and possibly more up-to-date) range of candidates. Both methods apply the same ranking function(s), as will be discussed below.

This paper will survey related work in Section 2 and introduce the expert-finding task in a university domain in Section 3. The process of ranking experts will be discussed in Section 4. The evaluation will be described in Section 4, followed by a discussion of the experiment's results in Section 5.

2 Related Work

The expert-finding task addresses the problem of retrieving a ranked list of people who are knowledgeable about a given topic. This task has found its place in the commercial environment as early as the 1980's, as discussed in Maybury (2006); however, there was very limited academic research on finding and ranking experts until the introduction of the enterprise track at the 2005 Text REtrieval Conference (TREC) (Craswell et al., 2005).

When expert-finding we must know the experts' profiles, These profiles may be generated manually or automatically. Manually created profiles may be problematic. If, for example, experts enter their own information, they may exaggerate or downplay their expertise. In addition, any changes of expertise for any expert requires a manual update to the expert's profile. Thus incurring high maintenance costs. An example of manually generated profiles is the work of Dumais and Nielsen (1992). Although their system automatically assigns submitted manuscripts to reviewers, the profiles of the reviewers or experts are created manually.

The alternative is to generate the profiles automatically, for example by extracting relevant information from a document collection. The assumption is that individuals will tend to be expert in the topics of documents with which they are associated. Experts can be associated with the documents in which they are mentioned (Craswell et al., 2001) or with e-mails they have sent or received (Balog and de Rijke, 2006a; Campbell et al., 2003; Dom et al., 2003). They can also be associated with their home pages or CVs (Maybury et al., 2001), and with documents they have written (Maybury et al., 2001; Becerra-Fernandez, 2000). Finally, some researchers use search logs to associate experts with the web pages they have visited (Wang et al., 2002; Macdonald and White, 2009).

After associating candidate experts with one or more of the kinds of textual evidence mentioned above, the next step is to find and rank candidates based on a user query. Many methods have been proposed to perform this task. Craswell et al. (2001) create virtual documents for each candidate (or employee). These virtual documents are simply concatenated texts of all documents from the corpus associated with a particular candidate. Afterwards, the system indexes and processes queries for the employee's documents. The results would show a list of experts based on the ten best matching employee documents. Liu et al. (2005) have applied expert-search in the context of a community-based question-answering service. Based on a virtual document approach, their work applied three language models: the query likelihood model, the relevance model and the cluster-based language model. They concluded that combining language models can enhance the retrieval performance.

Two principal approaches recognised for expert-finding can be found in the literature. Both were first proposed by Balog et al. (2006b). The models are called the candidate model and the document model, or Model 1 and Model 2, respectively. Different names have been used for the two methods. Fang and Zhai (2007) refer to them as 'Candidate Generation Models and Topic Generation Models'. Petkova and Croft (2006) call them the 'Query-Dependent Model' and the 'Query-Independent Model'. The main difference between the models is that the candidate-based approaches (Model 1) build a textual representation of candidate experts, and then rank the candidates based on the given query, whereas the document-based approaches (Model 2) first find documents that are relevant to the query, and then locate the associated experts in these documents.

Balog et al. (2006b) have compared the two models and concluded that Model 2 outperforms Model 1 on all measures (for this reason, we will adopt Model 2).

As Model 2 proved to be more efficient, it formed the basis of many other expert-search systems (Fang and Zhai, 2007; Petkova and Croft, 2007; Yao et al., 2008). Fang and Zhai developed a mixture model using proximity-based document representation. This model makes it possible to put different weights on different representations of a candidate expert (Fang and Zhai, 2007). Another mixture of personal and global language models was proposed by Serdyukov and Hiemstra (2008). They combined two criteria for personal expertise in the final ranking: the probability of generation of the query by the personal language model and a prior probability of candidate experts that expresses their level of activity in the important discussions on the query topic.

Zhu et al. (2010) claimed that earlier language models did not consider document features. They proposed an approach that incorporates: internal document structure; document URLs; page rank; anchor texts; and multiple levels of association between experts and topics.

All of the proposed frameworks assume that the more documents associated with a candidate that score highly with respect to a query, the more likely the candidate is to have relevant expertise for that query. Macdonald and Ounis (2008) developed a different approach, called the Voting Model. In their model, candidate experts are ranked first by considering a ranking of documents with respect to the users' query. Then, using the candidate profiles, votes from the ranked documents are converted into votes for candidates.

There have been attempts to tackle the expert-finding problem using social networks. This has mainly been investigated from two directions. The first direction uses graph-based measures on social networks to produce a ranking of experts (Campbell et al., 2003; Dom et al., 2003). The second direction assumes similarities among the neighbours in a social network and defines a smoothing procedure to rank experts (Karimzadehgan et al., 2009; Zhang et al., 2007).

Some have argued that it is not enough to find experts by looking only at the queries' without taking the users into consideration. They claim that there are several factors that may play a role in decisions concerning which experts to recommend. Some of these factors are the users' expertise level, social proximity and physical proximity (Borgatti and Cross, 2003; McDonald and Ackerman, 1998; Shami et al., 2008). McDonald and Ackerman (1998) emphasised the importance of the accessibility of the expert. They argued that people usually prefer to contact the experts who are physically or organisationally close to them. Moreover, Shami et al. (2008) found that people prefer to contact experts they know, even when they could potentially receive more information from other experts who are located outside their social network.

Woudstra and van den Hooff (2008) identified a number of factors in selecting experts that are related to quality and accessibility. They argued that the process of choosing which candidate expert to contact might differ depending on the specific situation.

Hofmann et al. (2010) showed that many of these factors can be modelled. They claimed that integrating them with retrieval models can improve retrieval performance. Smirnova and Balog (2011) provided a user-oriented model for expert-finding where they placed an emphasis on the social distance between the user and the expert. They considered a number of social graphs based on organisational hierarchy, geographical location and collaboration.

3 Expert-Finding in a University

In any higher educational institution, finding an appropriate supervisor is a critical task for research students, a task that can be very time consuming, especially if academics describe their work using terms that a student is not familiar with. A searcher may build up a picture of who is likely to have the relevant expertise by looking for university academic staff who have written numerous documents about the general topic, who have authored documents exactly related to the topic, or who list the topic as one of their research interest areas. Automating this process will not only help research students find the most suitable supervisors, but it also allow the university to allocate applications to supervisors, and help researchers find other people interested in the particular topics.

3.1 Method

The two approaches we apply, database-driven, and data-driven using NER[1] are illustrated in Figure 1.

[1]We use OpenNLP to identify named entities.

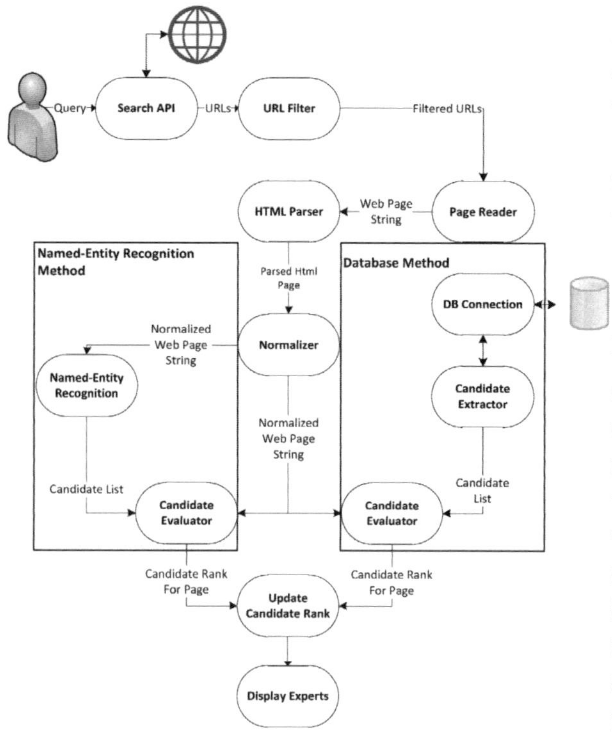

Figure 1: System Architecture.

The main difference between the two methods is the way in which the candidates' list is constructed. We argue that each method has its advantages. In the database method, the candidates are simply the university's academic staff. This avoids giving results unrelated to the university. It would be appropriate if the aim is to find the experts from among the university academics. In the data-driven method, the candidates are extracted from the pages returned by the underlying search engine. The experts found by this method are not necessarily university staff. They could be former academics, PhD students, visiting professors, or newly appointed staff.

Both methods apply the same ranking functions, one baseline function which is purely based on frequency and one which takes into account proximity of query terms with matches of potential candidates in the retrieved set of documents.

3.2 The Baseline Approach

The baseline we chose for ranking candidates is the frequency of appearance of names in the top twenty retrieved documents. The system counts how many times the candidate's name appears in the document $d(cc)$. Then it calculates the candidate metric cm by dividing the candidate count $d(cc)$ by the number of tokens in the document $d(nt)$.

Equation 1 defines the metric, where cm is the final candidate's metric for all documents and n is the number of documents.

$$cm = \sum_{d=1}^{n} \frac{d(cc)}{d(nt)} \qquad (1)$$

3.3 Our Approach

Our approach takes into account the proximity between query terms and candidate names in the matching documents in the form of a *distance weight*. This measure will adds a *distance weight* value to the main candidate's metric that was generated earlier. Similar approaches have been proposed in the literature for different expert search applications Lu et al. (2006); Cao et al. (2005). The *distance weight* will be higher whenever the name appears closer to the query term, within a +/- 10 word window.

We experiment with two different formulae. The first formula is as follows:

$$cm1 = \sum_{i=1}^{n}\sum_{j=1}^{m}(cm + \frac{1}{\beta * \alpha_{ij}}), \alpha_{ij} = \begin{cases} d_{ij} & \text{if } d_{ij} \leq 10 \\ 0 & \text{Otherwise} \end{cases} \qquad (2)$$

where n is the number of times the candidate's name has been found in the matching documents, m is the number of times the (full) query has been identified, and d_{ij} is the distance between the name position and query position (β has been set empirically to 3). The second formula is:

$$cm2 = \sum_{i=1}^{n}\sum_{j=1}^{m}(cm + \frac{1}{cm^{\alpha_{ij}}}), \alpha_{ij} = \begin{cases} d_{ij} & \text{if } d_{ij} \leq 10 \\ 0 & \text{Otherwise} \end{cases} \qquad (3)$$

This equation is designed to return a smaller value as the distance x increases, and to give the candidate with lower frequency a higher weight.

In both cases, candidates are ranked according to the final score and displayed in order so that the candidates who are most likely to be experts are displayed at the top of the list.

4 Evaluation

As with any IR system, evaluation can be difficult. In the given context one might argue that precision is more important than recall. In any case, recall can be difficult to measure precisely. To address these issues we approximate a *gold standard* as follows. We selected one school within the university for which a page of research topics with corresponding academics exists In this experiment we take this mapping as a complete set of correct matches. In this page, there are 371 topics (i.e. potential queries) divided among 28 more general research topics. Each topic/query is associated with one or more of the school's academic staff. It is presumed that those names belong to experts on the corresponding topics.

Table 1 illustrates some general topics with the number of (sub)topic they contain. Table 2 list some of the topics.

Topic	**N**
Analogue and Digital Systems Architectures	2
Artificial Intelligence	26
Audio	12
Brain Computer Interface	18
Computational Finance Economics and Management	1
Computational Intelligence	10
...	...

Table 1: Distribution of topics - **N** denotes the number of topics for the corresponding general topic area.

High-Speed Lasers And Photodetectors
Human Behaviour And The Psychology
Human Motion Tracking
Human-Centred Robotics
Hybrid Heuristics
Hybrid Intelligent Systems Which Include Neuro-Fuzzy Systems
Hypercomplex Algebras And Fourier Transforms
Hypercomplex Fourier Transforms And Filters

Table 2: Some topics/queries

The measure used to test the system is *recall* at the following values {3, 5, 7, 10, 15, 20}. We also measure Mean Average Precision at rank 20 (MAP@20).

5 Results and Discussion

Table 3 shows the system results where BL is the baseline result. There are two main findings. First of all, the database-driven approach outperforms the data-driven approach. Secondly, our approach which applies a grading of results based on proximity between queries and potential expert names significantly outperforms the baseline approach that only considers frequency, that is true for both formulae we apply when ranking the results (using paired t-tests applied to MAP with $p<0.0001$). However, the differences between $cm1$ and $cm2$ tend not to be significantly different.

	BL		$cm1$		$cm2$	
	NER	DB	NER	DB	NER	DB
R@3	0.47	0.48	0.49	0.76	0.58	0.79
R@5	0.56	0.60	0.58	0.83	0.68	0.86
R@7	0.61	0.64	0.62	0.87	0.72	0.88
R@10	0.65	0.69	0.68	0.89	0.78	0.90
R@15	0.69	0.72	0.74	0.91	0.80	0.91
R@20	0.71	0.75	0.76	0.92	0.82	0.93
MAP	0.20	0.28	0.50	0.61	0.52	0.66

Table 3: Performance Measures

It is perhaps important to mention that our data is fairly clean. More noise would make the creation of relational database more difficult. In that case the data-driven approach may become more appropriate.

6 Conclusion

The main objective of this work was to explore expert-finding in a university domain, an area that has to the best of our knowledge so far attracted little attention in the literature. The main finding is that a database-driven approach (utilising a fixed set of known experts) outperforms a data-driven approach which is based on automatic named-entity recognition. Furthermore, exploiting proximity between query and candidate outperforms a straight frequency measure.

There are a number of directions for future work. For example, modelling the user background and interests could increase the system's effectiveness. Some more realistic end-user studies could be used to evaluate the systems. Consideration could be given to term dependence and positional models as in Metzler and Croft (2005), which might improve our proximity-based scoring function. Finaly, our gold standard collection penalises a data-driven approach, which might offer a broader range of experts. We will continue this line of work using both technical evaluation measures as well as user-focused evaluations.

References

K. Balog and M. de Rijke. Finding experts and their details in e-mail corpora. In *Proceedings of the 15th international conference on World Wide Web*, pages 1035–1036. ACM, 2006a.

K. Balog, L. Azzopardi, and M. de Rijke. Formal models for expert finding in enterprise corpora. In *Proceedings of the 29th annual international ACM SIGIR conference on Research and development in information retrieval*, pages 43–50. ACM, 2006b.

I. Becerra-Fernandez. Facilitating the online search of experts at NASA using expert seeker people-finder. In *Proceedings of the 3rd International Conference on Practical Aspects of Knowledge Management (PAKM)*, Basel, Switzerland, 2000.

S.P. Borgatti and R. Cross. A relational view of information seeking and learning in social networks. *Management science*, 49(4):432–445, 2003.

C.S. Campbell, P.P. Maglio, A. Cozzi, and B. Dom. Expertise identification using email communications. In *Proceedings of the twelfth international conference on Information and knowledge management*, pages 528–531. ACM, 2003.

Y. Cao, J. Liu, S. Bao, and H. Li. Research on expert search at enterprise track of trec 2005. In *14th Text Retrieval Conference (TREC 2005)*, 2005.

N. Craswell, D. Hawking, A.M. Vercoustre, and P. Wilkins. P@ noptic expert: Searching for experts not just for documents. In *Ausweb Poster Proceedings, Queensland, Australia*, 2001.

N. Craswell, A.P. de Vries, and I. Soboroff. Overview of the TREC-2005 enterprise track. In *TREC 2005 Conference Notebook*, pages 199–205, 2005.

B. Dom, I. Eiron, A. Cozzi, and Y. Zhang. Graph-based ranking algorithms for e-mail expertise analysis. In *Proceedings of the 8th ACM SIGMOD workshop on Research issues in data mining and knowledge discovery*, pages 42–48. ACM, 2003.

S.T. Dumais and J. Nielsen. Automating the assignment of submitted manuscripts to reviewers. In *Proceedings of the 15th annual international ACM SIGIR conference on Research and development in information retrieval*, pages 233–244. ACM, 1992.

H. Fang and C.X. Zhai. Probabilistic models for expert finding. *Advances in Information Retrieval*, pages 418–430, 2007.

K. Hofmann, K. Balog, T. Bogers, and M. de Rijke. Contextual factors for finding similar experts. *Journal of the American Society for Information Science and Technology*, 61(5):994–1014, 2010.

M. Karimzadehgan, R. White, and M. Richardson. Enhancing expert finding using organizational hierarchies. *Advances in Information Retrieval*, pages 177–188, 2009.

C. Law and E. Ngai. An empirical study of the effects of knowledge sharing and learning behaviors on firm performance. *Expert Systems with Applications*, 34(4):2342–2349, 2008.

M. Li, L. Liu, and C. Li. An approach to expert recommendation based on fuzzy linguistic method and fuzzy text classification in knowledge management systems. *Expert Systems with Applications*, 38 (7):8586–8596, 2011.

X. Liu, W.B. Croft, and M. Koll. Finding experts in community-based question-answering services. In *Proceedings of the 14th ACM international conference on Information and knowledge management*, pages 315–316. ACM, 2005.

W. Lu, S. Robertson, A. MacFarlane, and H. Zhao. Window-based enterprise expert search. In *Proceeddings of the 15th Text REtrieval Conference (TREC 2006)*. NIST, 2006.

C. Macdonald and I. Ounis. Voting techniques for expert search. *Knowledge and information systems*, 16(3):259–280, 2008.

C. Macdonald and R.W. White. Usefulness of click-through data in expert search. In *SIGIR*, volume 9, pages 816–817, 2009.

M. Maybury, R. D'Amore, and D. House. Expert finding for collaborative virtual environments. *Communications of the ACM*, 44(12): 55–56, 2001.

M.T. Maybury. Expert finding systems. *MITRE Center for Integrated Intelligence Systems Bedford, Massachusetts, USA*, 2006.

D.W. McDonald and M.S. Ackerman. Just talk to me: a field study of expertise location. In *Proceedings of the 1998 ACM conference on Computer supported cooperative work*, pages 315–324. ACM, 1998.

D. Metzler and W.B. Croft. A markov random field model for term dependencies. In *Proceedings of the 28th annual international ACM SIGIR conference on Research and development in information retrieval*, pages 472–479. ACM, 2005.

I. Nonaka and H. Takeuchi. *The knowledge creating company: How Japanese The knowledge creating company: How Japanese companies create the dynamics of innovation*. Oxford University Press, New York, 1995.

D. Petkova and W.B. Croft. Hierarchical language models for expert finding in enterprise corpora. In *Tools with Artificial Intelligence, 2006. ICTAI'06. 18th IEEE International Conference on*, pages 599–608. IEEE, 2006.

D. Petkova and W.B. Croft. Proximity-based document representation for named entity retrieval. In *Proceedings of the sixteenth ACM conference on Conference on information and knowledge management*, pages 731–740. ACM, 2007.

P. Serdyukov and D. Hiemstra. Modeling documents as mixtures of persons for expert finding. *Advances in Information Retrieval*, pages 309–320, 2008.

N.S. Shami, K. Ehrlich, and D.R. Millen. Pick me: link selection in expertise search results. In *Proceeding of the twenty-sixth annual SIGCHI conference on Human factors in computing systems*, pages 1089–1092. ACM, 2008.

E. Smirnova and K. Balog. A user-oriented model for expert finding. *Advances in Information Retrieval*, pages 580–592, 2011.

J. Wang, Z. Chen, L. Tao, W.Y. Ma, and L. Wenyin. Ranking user's relevance to a topic through link analysis on web logs. In *Proceedings of the 4th international workshop on Web information and data management*, pages 49–54. ACM, 2002.

L. Woudstra and B. van den Hooff. Inside the source selection process: Selection criteria for human information sources. *Information Processing & Management*, 44(3):1267–1278, 2008.

K. Yang and S. Huh. Automatic expert identification using a text automatic expert identification using a text categorization technique in knowledge management systems. *Expert Systems with Expert Systems with Applications*, 34(2):1445–1455, 2008.

J. Yao, J. Xu, and J. Niu. Using role determination and expert mining in the enterprise environment. In *Proceedings of the 2008 Text REtrieval Conference (TREC 2008)*, 2008.

J. Zhang, J. Tang, and J. Li. Expert finding in a social network. *Advances in Databases: Concepts, Systems and Applications*, pages 1066–1069, 2007.

J. Zhu, X. Huang, D. Song, and S. Rüger. Integrating multiple document features in language models for expert finding. *Knowledge and Information Systems*, 23(1):29–54, 2010.

Automatic Animacy Classification

Samuel R. Bowman
Department of Linguistics
Stanford University
450 Serra Mall
Stanford, CA 94305-2150
sbowman@stanford.edu

Harshit Chopra
Department of Computer Science
Stanford University
353 Serra Mall
Stanford, CA 94305-9025
harshitc@stanford.edu

Abstract

We introduce the automatic annotation of noun phrases in parsed sentences with tags from a fine-grained semantic animacy hierarchy. This information is of interest within lexical semantics and has potential value as a feature in several NLP tasks.

We train a discriminative classifier on an annotated corpus of spoken English, with features capturing each noun phrase's constituent words, its internal structure, and its syntactic relations with other key words in the sentence. Only the first two of these three feature sets have a substantial impact on performance, but the resulting model is able to fairly accurately classify new data from that corpus, and shows promise for binary animacy classification and for use on automatically parsed text.

1 Introduction

An animacy hierarchy, in the sense of Zaenen et al. (2004), is a set of mutually exclusive categories describing noun phrases (NPs) in natural language sentences. These classes capture the degree to which the entity described by an NP is capable of human-like volition: a key lexical semantic property which has been shown to trigger a number of morphological and syntactic phenomena across languages. Annotating a corpus with this information can facilitate statistical semantic work, as well as providing a potentially valuable feature—discussed in Zaenen et al.—for tasks like relation extraction, parsing[1], and machine translation.

The handful of papers that we have found on animacy annotation—centrally Ji and Lin (2009), Øvrelid (2005), and Orasan and Evans (2001)—classify only the basic ANIMATE/INANIMATE contrast, but show some promise in doing so. Their work shows success in automatically classifying individual words, and related work has shown that animacy can be used to improve parsing performance (Øvrelid and Nivre, 2007).

We adopt the class set presented in Zaenen et al. (2004), and build our model around the annotated corpus presented in that work. Their hierarchy contains ten classes, meant to cover a range of categories known to influence animacy-related phenomena cross-linguistically. They are HUMAN, ORG (organizations), ANIMAL, MAC (automata), VEH (vehicles), PLACE, TIME, CONCRETE (other physical objects), NONCONC (abstract entities), and MIX (NPs describing heterogeneous groups of entities). The class definitions are straightforward—every NP describing a vehicle is a VEH—and Zaenen et al. offer a detailed treatment of ambiguous cases. Unlike the class sets used in named entity recognition work, these classes are crucially meant to cover all NPs. This includes freestanding nouns like *people*, as well as pronominals like *that one*, for which the choice of class often depends on contextual information not contained within the NP, or even the sentence.

In the typical case where the head of an NP belongs unambiguously to a single animacy class, the phrase as a whole nearly always takes on the class of its head: *The Panama hat I gave to my uncle on Tuesday* contains numerous nominals of differ-

[1] Using our model in parsing would require bootstrapping from c oarser parses, as our model makes use of some syntactic features.

Proceedings of the NAACL HLT 2012 Student Research Workshop, pages 7–10,
Montréal, Canada, June 3-8, 2012. ©2012 Association for Computational Linguistics

ent animacy classes, but *hat* is the unique syntactic head, and determines the phrase to be CONCRETE. Heads can easily be ambiguous, though: *My stereo speakers* and *the speakers at the panel session* belong to different classes, but share a (polysemous) head.

The corpus that we use is Zaenen et al.'s animacy-annotated subset of the hand-parsed Switchboard corpus of conversational American English. It is built on, and now included in, Calhoun et al.'s (2010) NXT version of Switchboard. This annotated section consists of about 110,000 sentences with about 300,000 NPs. We divide these sentences into a training set (80%), a development set (10%), and a test set (10%).[2] Every NP in this section is either assigned a class or marked as problematic, and we train and test on all the NPs for which the annotators were able to agree (after discussion) on an assignment.

2 Methods

We use a standard maximum entropy classifier (Berger et al., 1996) to classify constituents: For each labeled NP in the corpus, the model selects the locally most probable class. Our features are described in this section.

We considered features that required dependencies between consecutively assigned classes, allowing large NPs to depend on smaller NPs contained within them, as in conjoined structures. These achieved somewhat better coverage of the rare MIX class, but did not yield any gains in overall performance, and are not included in our results.

2.1 Bag-of-words features

Our simplest feature set, HASWORD-(*tag-*)*word*, simply captures each word in the NP, both with and without its accompanying part-of-speech (POS) tag.

2.2 Internal syntactic features

Motivated by the observation that syntactic heads tend to determine animacy class, we introduce two features: HEAD-*tag-word* contains the head word of the phrase (extracted automatically from the parse) and its POS tag. HEADSHAPE-*tag-shape* attempts to cover unseen head words by replacing the word string with its orthographic shape (substituting, for example, *Stanford* with Ll and *3G-related* with dL-l).

2.3 External syntactic features

The information captured by our tag set overlaps considerably with the information that verbs use to select their arguments.[3] The subject of *see*, for example, must be a HUMAN, MAC, ANIMAL, or ORG, and the complement of *above* cannot be a TIME. As such, we expect the verb or preposition that an NP depends upon and the type of dependency involved (subject, direct object, or prepositional complement) to be powerful predictors of animacy, and introduce the following features: SUBJ(-OF-*verb*), DOBJ(-OF-*verb*) and PCOMP(-OF-*prep*)(-WITH-*verb*). We extract these dependency relations from our parses, and mark an occurrence of each feature both with and without each of its optional (parenthetical) parameters.

3 Results

The following table shows our model's precision and recall (as percentages) for each class and the model's overall accuracy (the percent of labeled NPs which were labeled correctly), as well as the number of instances of each class in the test set.

Class	Count	Precision	Recall
VEH	534	88.56	39.14
TIME	1,101	88.24	80.38
NONCONC	12,173	83.39	93.32
MAC	79	63.33	24.05
PLACE	754	64.89	63.00
ORG	1,208	58.26	27.73
MIX	29	7.14	3.45
CONCRETE	1402	58.82	37.58
ANIMAL	137	69.44	18.25
HUMAN	11,320	91.19	93.30
Overall	28,737	Accuracy: 84.90	

The next table shows the performance of each feature bundle when it alone is used in classification, as well as the performance of the model when each

[2]We inadvertently did some initial feature selection using training data that included both our training and test sets. While we have re-run all of those experiments, this introduces a possible bias towards features which perform well on our test set.

[3]See Levin and Rappaport Hovav (2005) for a survey of argument selection criteria, including animacy.

feature bundle is excluded. We offer for comparison a baseline model that always chooses the most frequent class, NONCONC.

Only these features:	Accuracy (%)
Bag of words	83.04
Internal Syntactic	75.85
External Syntactic	50.35
All but these features:	—
Bag of words	77.02
Internal syntactic	83.36
External syntactic	84.58
Most frequent class	42.36
Full model	**84.90**

3.1 Binary classification

We test our model's performance on the somewhat better-known task of binary (ANIMATE/INANIMATE) classification by merging the model's class assignments into two sets after classification, following the grouping defined in Zaenen et al.[4] While none of our architectural choices were made with binary classification in mind, it is heartening to know that the model performs well on this easier task.

Overall accuracy is 93.50%, while a baseline model that labels each NP ANIMATE achieves only 53.79%. All of the feature sets contribute measurably to the binary model, and external syntactic features do much better on this task than on fine-grained classification, despite remaining the worst of the three sets: They achieve 78.66% when used alone. We have found no study on animacy in spoken English with which to compare these results.

3.2 Automatically parsed data

In order to test the robustness of our model to the errors introduced by an automatic parser, we train an instance of the Stanford parser (Klein and Manning, 2002) on our training data (which is relatively small by parsing standards), re-parse the linearized test data, and then train and test our classifier on the resulting trees.

Since we can only confidently evaluate classification choices for correctly parsed constituents, we consider accuracy measured only over those hypothesized NPs which encompass the same string of words as an NP in the gold standard data. Our parser generated correct (evaluable) NPs with precision 88.63% and recall 73.51%, but for these evaluable NPs, accuracy was marginally *better* than on hand-parsed data: 85.43% using all features. The parser likely tended to misparse those NPs which were hardest for our model to classify.

3.3 Error analysis

A number of the errors made by the model presented above stem from ambiguous cases where head words, often pronouns, can take on referents of multiple animacy classes, and where there is no clear evidence within the bounds of the sentence of which one is correct. In the following example the model incorrectly assigns *mine* the class CONCRETE, and nothing in the sentence provides evidence for the surprising correct class, HUMAN.

> Well, I've used *mine* on concrete treated wood.

For a model to correctly treat cases like this, it would be necessary to draw on a simple co-reference resolution system and incorporate features dependent on plausibly co-referent sentences elsewhere in the text.

The distinction between an organization (ORG) and a non-organized group of people (HUMAN) in this corpus is troublesome for our model. It hinges on whether the group shares a voice or purpose, which requires considerable insight into the meaning of a sentence to assess. For example, *people* in the below is an ORG, but no simple lexical or syntactic cues distinguish it from the more common class HUMAN.

> The only problem is, of course, that, uh, that requires significant commitment from *people* to actually decide they want to put things like that up there.

Our performance on the class MIX, which marks NPs describing multiple heterogeneous entities, was very poor. The highlighted NP in the sentence below was incorrectly classified NONCONC:

> But the same money could probably be far better spent on, uh, uh, *lunar bases and*

[4] HUMAN, VEH, MAC, ORG, ANIMAL, and HUMAN are considered animate, and the remaining classes inanimate.

solar power satellite research and, you know, so forth.

It is quite plausible that some more sophisticated approaches to modeling this unique class might be successful, but no simple feature that we tried had any success, and the effect of missing MIX on overall performance is negligible.

There are finally some cases where our attempts to rely on the heads of NPs were thwarted by the relatively flat structure of the parses. Under any mainstream theory of syntax, *home* is more prominent than *nursing* in the phrase *a nursing home*: It is the unique head of the NP. However, the parse provided does not attribute any internal structure to this constituent, making it impossible for the model to determine the relative prominence of the two nouns. Had the model known that the unique head of the phrase was *home*, it would have likely have correctly classified it as a PLACE, rather than the a priori more probable NONCONC.

4 Conclusion and future work

We succeeded in developing a classifier capable of annotating texts with a potentially valuable feature, with a high tolerance for automatically generated parses, and using no external or language-specific sources of knowledge.

We were somewhat surprised, though, by the relatively poor performance of the external syntactic features in this model: When tested alone, they achieved an accuracy of only about 50%. This signals one possible site for further development.

Should this model be used in a setting where external knowledge sources are available, two seem especially promising. Synonyms and hypernyms from WordNet (Fellbaum, 2010) or a similar lexicon could be used to improve the model's handling of unknown words—demonstrated successfully with the aid of a word sense disambiguation system in Orasan and Evans (2001) for binary animacy classification on single words. A lexical-semantic database like FrameNet (Baker et al., 1998) could also be used to introduce semantic role labels (which are tied to animacy restrictions) as features, potentially rescuing the intuition that governing verbs and prepositions carry animacy information.

Acknowledgments

We are indebted to Marie-Catherine de Marneffe and Jason Grafmiller, who first suggested we model this corpus, and to Chris Manning and our reviewers for valuable advice.

References

C.F. Baker, C.J. Fillmore, and J.B. Lowe. 1998. The Berkeley Framenet Project. In *Proc. of the 36th Annual Meeting of the Association for Computational Linguistics and 17th International Conference on Computational Linguistics.*

A.L. Berger, V.J Della Pietra, and S.A. Della Pietra. 1996. A maximum entropy approach to natural language processing. *Computational Linguistics*, 22(1).

S. Calhoun, J. Carletta, J.M. Brenier, N. Mayo, D. Jurafsky, M. Steedman, and D. Beaver. 2010. The NXT-format Switchboard Corpus. *Language resources and evaluation*, 44(4).

C. Fellbaum. 2010. Wordnet. In *Theory and Applications of Ontology: Computer Applications*. Springer.

H. Ji and D. Lin. 2009. Gender and animacy knowledge discovery from web-scale N-grams for unsupervised person mention detection. *Proc. of the 23rd Pacific Asia Conference on Language, Information and Computation.*

D. Klein and C.D. Manning. 2002. Fast exact inference with a factored model for natural language parsing. *Advances in neural information processing systems*, 15(2002).

B. Levin and M. Rappaport Hovav. 2005. *Argument Realization*. Cambridge.

C. Orasan and R. Evans. 2001. Learning to identify animate references. *Proc. of the Workshop on Computational Natural Language Learning*, 7.

L. Øvrelid and J. Nivre. 2007. When word order and part-of-speech tags are not enough—Swedish dependency parsing with rich linguistic features. In *Proc. of the International Conference on Recent Advances in Natural Language Processing.*

Lilja Øvrelid. 2005. Animacy classification based on morphosyntactic corpus frequencies: some experiments with Norwegian nouns. In *Proc. of the Workshop on Exploring Syntactically Annotated Corpora.*

A. Zaenen, J. Carletta, G. Garretson, J. Bresnan, A. Koontz-Garboden, T. Nikitina, M.C. O'Connor, and T. Wasow. 2004. Animacy encoding in English: why and how. In *Proc. of the Association for Computational Linguistics Workshop on Discourse Annotation.*

Beauty Before Age?
Applying Subjectivity to Automatic English Adjective Ordering

Felix Hill
Dept. of Theoretical & Applied Linguistics
and Computer Laboratory
University of Cambridge
Cambridge CB3 9DA, UK
fh295@cam.ac.uk

Abstract

The preferred order of pre-nominal adjectives in English is determined primarily by semantics. Nevertheless, Adjective Ordering (AO) systems do not generally exploit semantic features. This paper describes a system that orders adjectives with significantly above-chance accuracy (73.0%) solely on the basis of semantic features pertaining to the cognitive-semantic dimension of *subjectivity*. The results indicate that combining such semantic approaches with current methods could result in more accurate and robust AO systems.

1 Introduction

As a significant body of linguistic research has observed (see e.g. Quirk et al. (1985)), English pre-nominal adjective strings exhibit subtle order restrictions. Although example (2), below, does not represent a clear-cut violation of established grammatical principles, it would sound distinctly unnatural to native speakers in the majority of contexts, in contrast to the entirely unproblematic (1).

(1) He poked it with a long metal fork
(2) ? He poked it with a metal long fork

The problem of determining the principles that govern Adjective Ordering (henceforth, AO) in English has been studied from a range of academic perspectives, including philosophy, linguistics, psychology and neuroscience. AO is also of interest in the field of Natural Language Processing (NLP), since a method that consistently selects felicitous orders would serve to improve the output of language modeling and generation systems.

Previous NLP approaches to AO infer the ordering of adjective combinations from instances of the same, or superficially similar, combinations in training corpora (Shaw & Hatzivassiloglou, 1999) (Malouf, 2000), or from distributional tendencies of the adjectives in multiple-modifier strings (Mitchell, 2009) (Dunlop, Mitchell, & Roark, 2010). Such methods are susceptible to data sparseness, since the combinations from which they learn are rare in everyday language.

By contrast, the approach taken here determines AO based on semantic features of adjectives, guided by the theoretical observation that the cognitive notion of *subjectivity* governs ordering in the general case (Adamson, 2000). The semantic features developed are each highly significant predictors of AO, and they combine to classify combinations with 73.0% accuracy. These preliminary results indicate that semantic AO systems can perform comparably to existing systems, and that classifiers exploiting semantic and direct evidence might surpass the current best-performing systems.

2 Previous research

The subtle nature of human ordering preferences makes AO a particularly challenging NLP task. In perhaps the first specific attempt to address the problem, Shaw and Hatzivassiloglou (1999) apply a *direct evidence* method. For a given adjective combination in the test data, their system searches a training corpus and selects the most frequent ordering of that combination. Because there is no basis to determine the order of adjective combinations that are not in the training data, Shaw and Hatzivassiloglou extend the domain of the classifi-

Proceedings of the NAACL HLT 2012 Student Research Workshop, pages 11–16,
Montréal, Canada, June 3-8, 2012. ©2012 Association for Computational Linguistics

er by assuming transitivity in the order relation, increasing the coverage with only a small reduction in accuracy. Nevertheless, the system remains highly dependent on the domain and quantity of training data. For example, accuracy is 92% when training and test data are both within the medical domain but only 54% in cross-domain contexts.

Malouf (2000) combines a direct evidence approach with an alternative method for extending the domain of his classifier. His system infers the order of unseen combinations from 'similar' seen combinations, where similarity is defined purely in terms of morphological form. The method works by exploiting a degree of correlation between form and order (e.g. capital letters indicate nominal modifiers, which typically occur to the right).

Mitchell (2009) applies a less 'direct' approach, clustering adjectives based on their position in multiple-modifier strings. Although Mitchell's classifier requires no direct evidence, data sparseness is still an issue because the strings from which the system learns are relatively infrequent in everyday language. Dunlop et al. (2010) apply Multiple Sequence Alignment (MSA), a statistical technique for automatic sequence ordering, which, as with Malouf's system, quantifies word-similarity based solely on morphological features. Despite the greater sophistication of these more recent approaches, Mitchell et al. (2011) showed that a simple n-gram (direct evidence) classifier trained on 170 million words of New York Times and Wall Street Journal text and tested on the Brown Corpus (82.3% accuracy) outperforms both the clustering (69.0%) and MSA (81.8%) methods.

Wulff (2003) uses Linear Discriminant Analysis (LDA) to quantify the effects of various potential AO correlates, and confirms that semantic features are better predictors than morphological and syntactic features. The features, extracted from the 10-million word Spoken British National Corpus (BNC) and weighted by LDA, combine to predict unseen adjective orders with 72% accuracy.

Wulff's study is unique in applying semantics to the problem, although her focus is theoretical and several features are implemented manually. The next section describes the theoretical basis for a fully-automated semantic approach to AO that could help to resolve the issues of data sparsity and domain dependence associated with the direct evidence methods described above.

2.1 The subjectivity hypothesis

Although phonetic, morphological and syntactic factors influence AO in specific contexts, there is consensus in the theoretical literature that semantics is the determining factor in the general case (see Quirk et al. (1985) for further discussion). Several semantic theories of AO make use of the cognitive linguistic notion of *subjectivity* (Quirk et al. 1985; Hetzron, 1978; Adamson 2000). Subjectivity in this context refers to the degree to which an utterance can or cannot be interpreted independently of the speaker's perspective (Langacker, 1991). For example, the deictic utterance (3) is more subjective than (4) since its truth depends on the speaker's location at the time of utterance.

(3) James is sitting across the table
(4) James is sitting opposite Sam

In relation to AO, Quirk et al, Hetzron and Adamson each support some form of the *subjectivity hypothesis:* that more subjective modifiers generally occur to the left of less subjective modifiers in pre-nominal strings. For example, in (5) the adjective *big* tells us about the relation between the car and the speaker's idea of typical car size. This ascription is less objectively verifiable than that of car color, so *big* occurs further from the head noun. The position of *oncoming* in (6) reflects the high inherent subjectivity of deictic modifiers.

(5) A big red Italian car (BNC)
(6) An oncoming small black car (BNC)

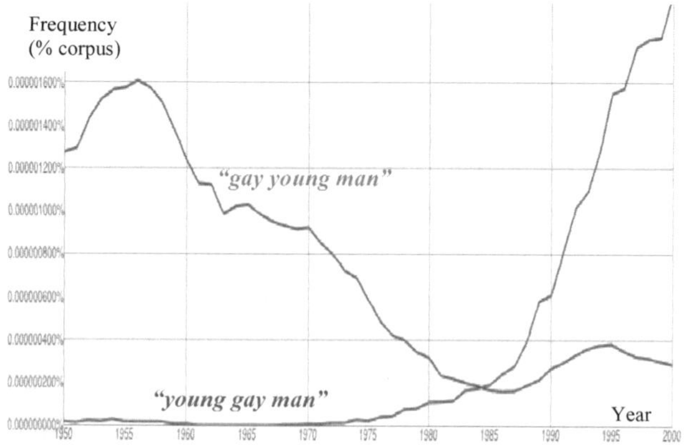

Figure 1: Diachronic variation of preferred AO

To illustrate a process of changing AO preferences that can be explained in a compelling way by the subjectivity hypothesis, the 1 trillion-word Google n-Gram Viewer was queried (Figure 1). The two lines indicate the frequency of the strings *'gay young man'* and *'young gay man'* in the Corpus from 1950 to 2000, as the pre-eminent meaning of *gay* evolved from the subjective *merry* to the categorical, well-defined *homosexual*. As the graph shows, this reduction in subjectivity has been accompanied by a marked increase in the tendency of *gay* to appear closer to the noun in such strings.

3 System design

The AO system described below applies the theoretical findings presented above by extracting from training data various subjectivity features of adjectives and applying this information to classify input orderings as correct or incorrect.[1] System operation and evaluation consisted of 5 stages.

Extracting feature profiles: The 200 highest-frequency adjectives in the BNC were extracted. Following Wulff (2003, p. 6), three items, *other*, *only* and *very* were removed from this list because they occur in right-branching structures. For the remaining adjectives, a 'profile' of feature values (c.f. Table 1, below), was extracted from 24 million words (*Sections A-C*) of the written BNC.

Generating gold-standard orderings: From the 197 adjectives, 19,306 unordered pairs $\{A_1, A_2\}$ were generated. The bigram frequencies of the strings $[A_1, A_2]$ and $[A_2, A_1]$ were then extracted from the 1 billion-word Google n-gram Corpus. From this data, the 12,000 pairs $\{A_1, A_2\}$ with the largest proportional difference in frequency between $[A_1, A_2]$ and $[A_2, A_1]$ were selected.

Defining test and training sets: A set of 12,000 ordered triples $[A_1, A_2, \delta_{[A_1, A_2]}]$ was generated, where $\delta_{[A_1, A_2]}$ is an indicator function taking the value 1 if $[A_1, A_2]$ is the preferred ordering in the Google corpus and 0 if $[A_2, A_1]$ is preferred. Some of the triples were re-ordered at random to leave an equal number of preferred and dispreferred orderings in the data. These triples were populated with feature profiles, to create vectors

$$[f_1^{A_1}, \ldots, f_n^{A_1}, f_1^{A_2}, \ldots f_n^{A_2}, \delta_{[A_1, A_2]}]$$

where $f_k^{A_i}$ is the value of the kth feature of the adjective A_i, and n is the total number of features. The set of vectors was then randomly partitioned in the ratio 80:20 for training and testing respectively.

Training the classifier: A logistic regression was applied to the set of training vectors, in which the first *2n* elements of the vectors were independent variables and the final element was the dependent variable. Logistic regression has been shown to be preferable to alternatives such as Ordinary Least Squares and LDA for binary outcome classification if, as in this case, the independent variables are not normally distributed (Press & Wilson, 1978).

Evaluation: Performance was determined by the number of pairs in the test data correctly ordered by the classifier. Steps 3-5 were repeated 4 times (5-fold cross-validation), with the scores averaged.

3.1 The Features

Of the features included in the model, COMPARABILITY and POLARITY are shown to correlate with human subjectivity judgments by Wiebe and colleagues (see e.g. Hatzivassiloglou & Wiebe, 2000). The remainder are motivated by observations in the theoretical literature.

MODIFIABILITY: Gradable adjectives, such as *hot* or *happy*, tend to be more subjective than prototypically categorical adjectives, such as *square* or *black* (Hetzron, 1978). Unlike categorical adjectives they admit modification by intensifiers (Paradis, 1997). Therefore, the feature MODIFIABILITY is defined as the conditional probability that an adjective occurs immediately following an intensifier given that it occurs at all.[2]

$$Modifiability(A) = \frac{\sum_{m \in M} freq([m, A])}{freq(A)}$$

$M = \{degree\ modifiers\}$
$[x, y]$ *is the bigram 'word x followed by word y'*

COMPARABILITY: Gradable adjectives also have comparative and superlative forms, whereas prototypically categorical adjectives do not. Given the association between gradability and subjectivity, the feature COMPARABILITY is defined as the probability of an adjective occurring in comparative or superlative form given it occurs at all.

[1] The system operates on adjectival and nominal modifiers but not on articles, determiners, degree modifiers and other non-adjectival pre-modifiers.

[2] The set of intensifiers is taken from (Paradis, 1997).

$$Comparability(A) = \frac{freq(\bar{A}) + freq(\bar{\bar{A}})}{freq(A) + freq(\bar{A}) + freq(\bar{\bar{A}})}$$

$\bar{A} = comparative\ form\ of\ A \quad \bar{\bar{A}} = superlative\ form\ of\ A$

PREDICATIVITY: Adjectives can be applied in both attributive (*'the red car'*), and predicative (*'the car is red'*) constructions. Bolinger (1967) suggests that predicative constructions are conceptualized more dynamically or temporarily than attributive constructions. Since dynamic properties are generally ascribed more subjectively than permanent properties (Langacker, 1991), Bolinger's intuition implies an association between subjectivity and predicative constructions. Indeed, many objective modifiers sit uncomfortably in predicative contexts, as shown by (7) and (8).

(7) I live in a brick house
(8) ? The house I live in is brick

The feature PREDICATIVITY is therefore defined as the probability that an adjective occurs in a predicative construction given that it occurs at all. The measure is implemented by counting the number of times the adjective immediately follows some form of an English copula verb.[3]

$$Predicativiy(A) = \frac{\sum_{c \in C} freq([c, A])}{freq(A)}$$

$C = set\ of\ English\ copula\ verbs\ in\ all\ inflected\ forms$

POLARITY: An adjective is said to be *polar* if it typically attributes a positive (*kind, healthy, strong*) or negative (*poor, selfish, rotten*) characteristic. Semi-supervised methods for automatically detecting adjective polarity have been developed (Hatzivassiloglou & McKeown, 1997), and applied to subjectivity analysis by Wiebe (2000). POLARITY is implemented as a binary feature, whose value depends on whether or not the adjective appears in a list of 1,300 polar adjectives extracted by Hatzivassiloglou & Mackeown.

$$Polarity(A) = \begin{cases} 1 & if\ A \in \boldsymbol{P} \cup \boldsymbol{N} \\ 0 & if\ A \notin \boldsymbol{P} \cup \boldsymbol{N} \end{cases}$$

$\boldsymbol{P} = \{\ adjectives\ labelled\ as\ positive\}$
$\boldsymbol{N} = \{adjectives\ labelled\ as\ negative\}$

[3] The copula verbs list was compiled manually by the author.

ADVERBIABILITY: Quirk (1985, p 1339) notes that evaluative adjectives tend to develop derived adverbial forms, whereas more objective adjectives do not. For example, *nice*, *beautiful* and, *careful* correspond to the adverbs *nicely*, *beautifully*, and *carefully*, whereas no such derived forms exist for the more objective adjectives *male*, *English* and *brown*. The ADVERBIABILITY of an adjective is defined as the ratio of derived adverbial forms to total base and adverbial forms in the corpus.

$$Adverbiability(A) = \frac{freq(A^*)}{freq(A) + freq(A^*)}$$

$A^* = adverbial\ form\ derived\ from\ A$

NOMINALITY: Wulff (2003) reports statistical evidence that more 'noun-like' modifiers appear closer to the head in modifying strings. Combinations such as *'bread knife'* or *'police car'*, often analyzed as noun-noun compounds rather than modifier/noun combinations, represent the clearest such examples. Amongst more prototypical adjectives, some, such as *green*, or *male* have nominal senses (*'village green'*, *'unidentified male'*), whereas others do not. Separately, Hatzivassiloglou and Wiebe (2000) report a statistical correlation between the number of adjectives in a text and human judgments of subjectivity. These observations suggest that adjectives are inherently more subjective than nouns, and further that noun-like 'behavior' might indicate relative objectivity within the class of adjectives. Consequently, the feature NOMINALITY is defined, following Wulff, as the probability that an adjective is tagged as a noun given that it is tagged as either an adjective or a noun. It is the only feature that is expected to exhibit an inverse correlation with subjectivity.

$$Nominality(A) = \frac{freq(A_n)}{freq(A_a) + freq(A_n)}$$

$A_n = adjective\ A\ tagged\ as\ noun$
$A_a = adjective\ A\ tagged\ as\ adjective$

	new	*good*	*old*	*different*	*local*
MODIF	0.0010	0.0529	0.0208	0.0887	0.0004
COM	0.0079	0.4881	0.2805	0.0011	0.0045
PRED	0.0100	0.1018	0.0289	0.0806	0.0069
POL	0.0000	1.0000	0.0000	0.0000	0.0000
ADV	0.0220	0.0008	0.0000	0.0318	0.0478
NOM	0.2900	0.0999	0.0113	0.0000	0.0212

Table 1: Example feature profiles

4 Results

The performance of the classifier is promising with respect to the intuition that semantic features can be usefully applied to AO systems. A chi-square test reveals the features collectively to be highly significant predictors of AO ($\chi^2 = 2257.25,\ p < 0.001^{***}$). Once trained, the system orders unseen combinations in the test data with accuracy of 73.0%, as detailed in Table 2. This figure is not directly comparable with previous work because of differences in the evaluation framework.

Observed		Predicted		
		Training Data		
		Incorrect	Correct	% Correct
	Incorrect	2773	1637	62.9
	Correct	1120	4101	78.5
	Overall%			71.4
		Test Data		
		Incorrect	Correct	% Correct
	Incorrect	696	370	65.3
	Correct	270	1031	79.2
	Overall%			73.0

Table 2: Overall results of model cross-validation

It is notable that the accuracy of the classifier rises to 86.2% when the test data is hand-picked as the 3000 pairs for which the strength of ordering preference is highest.[4] This suggests that the approach could be particularly effective at detecting highly unnatural combinations. Moreover, the performance when tested on the 3000 (unseen) pairs with the lowest ordering preference is 70.1%, indicating the potential to cope well with marginal cases and rare combinations.

As Table 3 shows, all features apart from COMPARABILITY are statistically significant predictors in the model ($p < 0.001^{***}$). In addition, the mean value of each feature over adjectives in first position A_1 differs significantly from the mean over adjectives in second position A_2 ($t \geq 28.07$ in each case, $df = 11{,}283$). Whilst relatively the weakest predictor, COMPARABILITY in isolation does predict AO at above-chance cy ($58.7\%,\ p < 0.001^{***}$)

. Its low significance in the overall model reflects its high level of interaction with other features; in particular, MODIFIABILITY (Pearson Correlation: .367, $p < 0.001^{***}$). The relative magnitude of the model coefficients is not informative, since the measurement scale is not common to all features. Nevertheless, the negative regression coefficient of NOMINALITY confirms that this feature correlates inversely with distance from the noun.

Feature	Regression Coefficient	Predictor Significance	Performance in Isolation	Comparison of A_1 / A_2 Means
MODIF	5.205	.000	62.9%	0.000
COM	.177	.381	58.7%	0.000
PRED	3.630	.000	68.6%	0.000
POL	.339	.000	60.4%	0.000
ADV	1.503	.000	62.8%	0.000
NOM	-.405	.000	58.4%	0.000

Table 3: Influence of individual features

To test the influence of the training corpus size on system performance, features were extracted from BNC *Section A* (7 million words) rather than *Sections A-C* (24 million words) in a separate experiment. This adjustment resulted in a reduction in classifier accuracy from 73.0% to 71.4%, indicating that performance could be significantly improved by training on the full BNC or even larger corpora. Further improvements could be achieved through the combination of semantic and 'direct' features. To illustrate this, the feature LEFTTENDENCY, a measure of the likelihood that an adjective occurs immediately to the left of another adjective in the training data, was added. This adjustment raised the classifier accuracy from 73.0% to 76.3%. It should also be noted that many of the features in the current system are extracted via measures that approximate syntactic dependency with bigram context. It is an empirical question whether the additional complexity associated with more precise measures (for example, applying dependency parsing) would be justified by performance improvements.

[4] The 3000 pairs for which the proportional preference for one ordering over another in the Google n-Gram corpus is highest and for which the total frequency of the pair exceeds 500.

5 Conclusion

This paper has tested the efficacy of applying automatic subjectivity quantification to the problem of AO. The reported results highlight the utility of such semantically oriented approaches. Although direct comparison with existing systems was beyond the scope of this study, exploratory analyses suggested that a refined version of this system might compare favorably with reported benchmarks, if trained on a corpus of comparable size.

Nevertheless, the comparatively weak performance of the present system on previously seen examples ('underfitting', see Table 2) is strong evidence that six features alone are insufficient to capture the complexity of ordering patterns. Therefore, beyond the adjustments discussed above, the next stage in this research will evaluate the effects of combining semantic features with direct evidence in a single system. Other future work might apply subjectivity features to cluster adjectives into classes pertinent to AO, perhaps in combination with independent distributional measures of semantic similarity. Finally, the approach presented here for English AO could have applications across languages, and may also be applicable to related tasks, such as ordering binomials[5], parsing noun phrases ('*wild animal hunt*' vs. '*wild birthday party*') and selecting thematically appropriate modifiers for a given head noun.

Some interesting theoretical insights also emerge as a corollary to the results of this study. The supposition that gradability, polarity, adverbiability, predicativity and 'nouniness' can be associated, either positively or negatively, with subjectivity, was confirmed. Moreover, the performance of the classifier lends support to the status of subjectivity as a determining principle of AO, and an important dimension of adjective semantics in general. As such, the reason we say *beautiful English rose*, (c.240,000 direct matches on Google) and not *English beautiful rose* (c.2,730) is because beauty is in the eye of the beholder, whereas nationality, evidently, is not.

[5] Binomials are noun or adjective combinations separated by coordinating conjunctions, such as *tired and emotional* and *salt and pepper*. Quirk et al. (1985, p. 1342) observe connections between binomial ordering and AO.

Acknowledgments

Thanks to Anna Korhonen, Paula Buttery and Sylvia Adamson for helpful guidance and comments.

References

Adamson, S. 2000. Word Order Options and Category Shift in the Premodifying String. In O. Fischer, *Pathways of Change: Grammaticalization in English* (pp. 39-66). Amsterdam: John Benjamins.

Bolinger, D. 1967. Adjectives in English: Attribution and Predication. *Lingua 18* , 1-34.

Dunlop, A., Mitchell, M. & Roark, B. 2010. Prenominal Modifier Ordering via Multiple Sequence Alignment. *2010 Annual Conference of the North American Chapter of the ACL (HLT-NAACL 2010).*

Hatzivassiloglou, V. & McKeown, K. 1997. Predicting the Semantic Orientation of Adjectives. *Annual Meeting Assoc. Comp.Ling. ACL '97,* 174-181.

Hatzivassiloglou, V. & Wiebe, J. 2000. Effects of Adjective Orientation and Gradability on Sentence Subjectivity. *International Conference on Computational Linguistics, COLING- '00.*

Hetzron, R. 1978. On the Relative Order of Adjectives. In I. H. (Ed.), *Language Universals.* Tübingen: Narr.

Langacker, R. 1991. *Foundations of Cognitive Grammar.* Stanford, CA: Stanford University Press.

Malouf, R. 2000. The Order of Prenominal Adjectives in Natural Language Generation. *Proc. 38th Annual Meeting, Assoc. Comp. Linguistics, ACL '00*, 85–92.

Mitchell, M. 2009. Class-based Ordering of Prenominal Modifiers. *Proc.12th European Workshop, Nat.Lang. Generation, ENLG '09*, 50–57.

Mitchell, M. Dunlop, A. & Roark, B. 2011. Semi-Supervised Modeling for Prenominal Modifier Ordering. *Proc. 49th Annual Meeting of the Assoc. Comp. Ling., ACL '11,* 236–241.

Paradis, C. 1997. *Degree Modifiers of Adjectives in Spoken British English.* Lund: Lund University Press.

Press, S. J. & Wilson, S. 1978. Choosing Between Logistic Regression and Discriminant Analysis. *Journal of American Statistical Association*, 699-705.

Quirk, R. Greenbaum, A. Leech, G. & Svartvik, J. 1985. *A Comprehensive Grammar of the English Language.* London: Longmans.

Shaw, J. & Hatzivassiloglou, V. 1999. Ordering Among Premodifiers. *Proc. 37th Annual Meeting, Association of Computational Linguistics, ACL '99* , 135–143.

Wiebe, J. 2000. Learning Subjective Adjectives from Corpora. *Proc. 17th National Conference on Artificial Intelligence (AAAI-2000).*

Wulff, S. 2003. A Multifactorial Analysis of Adjective Order in English. *International Journal of Corpus Linguistics*, 245–282.

Indexing Google 1T for low-turnaround wildcarded frequency queries

Steinar Vittersø Kaldager
University of Oslo, Department of Informatics
steinavk@ifi.uio.no

Abstract

We propose a technique to prepare the Google 1T n-gram data set for wildcarded frequency queries with a very low turnaround time, making unbatched applications possible. Our method supports token-level wildcarding and – given a cache of 3.3 GB of RAM – requires only a single read of less than 4 KB from the disk to answer a query. We present an indexing structure, a way to generate it, and suggestions for how it can be tuned to particular applications.

1 Background and motivation

The "Google 1T" data set (LDC #2006T13) is a collection of 2-, 3-, 4-, and 5-gram frequencies extracted at Google from around 10^{12} tokens of raw web text. Wide access to web-scale data being a relative novelty, there has been considerable interest in the research community in how this resource can be put to use (Bansal and Klein, 2011; Hawker et al., 2007; Lin et al., 2010, among others).

We are concerned with facilitating approaches where a large number of frequency queries (optionally with token-by-token wildcarding) are made automatically in the context of a larger natural language-based system. Our motivating example is Bansal and Klein (2011) who substantially improve statistical parsing by integrating frequency-based features from Google 1T, taken as indicative of associations between words. In this work, however, parser test data is preprocessed "off-line" to make n-gram queries tractable, hampering the practical utility of this work. Our technique eliminates such barriers to application, making it feasible to answer previously unseen wildcarded frequency queries "on-line", i.e. when parsing new inputs. We devise a structure to achieve this, making each query approximately the cost of a single random disk access, using an in-memory cache of about 3 GB.

Our own implementation will be made available to other researchers as open source.

2 Prior work

Sekine and Dalwini (2010) have built a high-quality "1T search engine" that can return lists of n-gram/frequency pairs matching various types of patterns, but they operate on a wider scale of queries that makes their reported performance ($0.34\,s$ per query) insufficient for our desired use.

Hawker, Gardiner and Bennetts (2007) have explored the same problem and devised a "lossy compression" strategy, deriving from the data set a lookup table fitting in RAM indexed by hashes of entries, with cells corresponding to more than one entry in the n-gram set filled with a "compromise" value appropriate to the application. Although they obtain very fast queries, in our estimation the error introduced by this method would be problematic for our desired use. Furthermore, the authors do not address wildcarding for this strategy.

Talbot and Osborne (2007b; 2007a) have explored applications of Bloom filters to making comparatively small probabilistic models of large n-gram data sets. Though their method too is randomized and subject to false positives, they discuss ways of controlling the error rate.

Finally, several researchers including Bansal and Klein (2011) and Hawker, Gardiner and Bennetts (2007) describe ways of working "off-line", without low-turnaround querying. However, systems built along these lines will be unable to efficiently solve single small problems as they arise.

3 The indexing structure

The Google 1T data set consists of entries for n-grams for $n \in \{1, 2, 3, 4, 5\}$. We have not ap-

Proceedings of the NAACL HLT 2012 Student Research Workshop, pages 17–22,
Montréal, Canada, June 3-8, 2012.

plied our methods to the unigrams, as these are few enough in number that they can be held in RAM and structured by a standard method such as a hash table.

For the n-grams for $n \in \{2, 3, 4, 5\}$, we use separate carefully tuned and generated B-trees(Bayer and McCreight, 1972), caching nodes near the root in RAM and keeping the rest on disk.

3.1 Preprocessing

We apply *preprocessing* to the Google 1T data in two ways. Firstly, in almost any application of Google 1T it will be desirable to perform preprocessing to discard unimportant details, both in order to obtain a more manageable set of data and to make patterns evident that would otherwise be obscured by data scarcity. We identify and collapse to class tokens IP addresses, email addresses, prefixed hexadecimal numbers, and various kinds of URIs. We also collapse all decimal numeric data by mapping all *digits* to the digit zero.

The preprocessing we apply (which is used to generate the data set described in the rest of this article) reduces the vocabulary size by about 37.6%. It is our belief that, seen as a whole, this preprocessing is quite mild, considering the amount of almost universally unnecessary detail in the input data (e.g. 26% of the "words" begin with a digit).

Secondly, we use preprocessing in an entirely different way, as a brute-force approach to supporting wildcarded queries. The lookup structure constructed does *not* provide any wildcarding features – instead we use the preprocessing phase to add entries for each of the 2^n possible variously-wildcarded queries (all the possible configurations with each position either wildcarded or not) matching each of the n-grams in the data.

After this preprocessing, the wildcard token $<\!*\!>$ can be treated just like any other token.

3.2 Dictionary

For cheaper processing and storage, our indexing structure deals in integers, not string tokens. The components of the structure describing this mapping are the *dictionaries*. These are associative arrays that are kept in RAM at runtime.

The main dictionary uniquely maps preprocessed tokens to integers (e.g., `<EMAIL>` $\longrightarrow$ 137). There are fewer than 2^{24} unique tokens in the 1T data set, so each integer requires only 3 bytes of storage.

During generation of the structure, we have found a second "transforming" dictionary useful. This dictionary maps *unpreprocessed* tokens to integers, e.g., `john@example.com` $\longrightarrow$ 137, avoiding string processing entirely. Unlike the normal dictionary, the transforming dictionary describes a many-to-one mapping.

The dictionaries are stored on disk simply as text files, with one line for each key/value pair. The appropriate dictionary is preloaded into an appropriate in-memory Judy array (Baskins, 2004) during initialization, taking up around 300 MB of memory.

The main and the transforming dictionaries have around 8 and 13 million entries respectively.

3.3 Search tree

Our central structure is a search tree, with the keys being fixed-length sequences of integer tokens.

Owing to the static nature of the data set, the tree can be constructed whole. For this reason there is no need to support insertions or deletions, and we do not account for them. Apart from the lack of support for mutation, the structure is a conventional B-tree (Bayer and McCreight, 1972). Our main contribution is identifying what sort of B-tree solves our problem, describing how it can be implemented effectively, and how it practically can be generated when dealing with a very large number of entries.

The tree should be broad to account for the difference in speed between searching within an in-memory node and retrieving the next node from disk. We use a branching factor limit of 127. With parameters like ours the tree will generally have a height (counting the root and the leaves, but not individual n-gram entries) of 5. It will be about half-filled, meaning – due to the generation method outlined in Subsection 4.3 – that the root will have around $\frac{127}{2}$ children. Figure 2 illustrates the pattern – rightmost nodes may have fewer children.

A larger node size for the leaves would mean lower memory requirements at the cost of having to make larger reads from the disk.

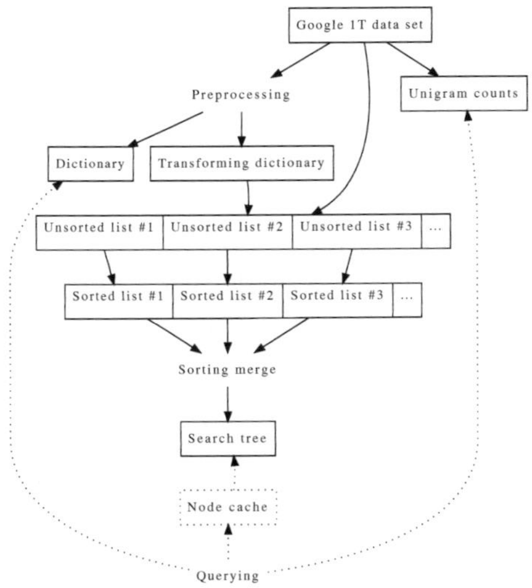

Figure 1: An overview of the steps involved in generating the indexing structure. The dotted portions indicate how it is later used.

4 Generating the structure

4.1 Creating the dictionaries

The dictionaries are created by simply iterating through the 1T vocabulary file, preprocessing and assigning integral labels.

During development we have performed it in Python and in Common Lisp, with the complexity of the preprocessing being on the order of 8 class-recognizer regular expressions and a character replacement pass for digits. One pass over the vocabulary with this setup takes around 18 minutes.

4.2 Creating sorted partial lists

We now seek to generate all the entries to be entered into our structure, ordered lexicographically by the numeric n-tuples that constitute the entry keys.

However, preprocessing portions of the (sorted) raw data set disturbs its ordering and introduces duplicate keys. After wildcarding it is also a concern that the list is very long – about $3.5 \cdot 10^{10}$ entries for the 5-grams after wildcarding and before merging.

As directly sorting a list of this size is impractical, we use an external sorting (Knuth, 1998) technique, dividing the input of length N into sections of K entries, then sort and merge duplicates in each one *separately*, producing $\lceil \frac{N}{K} \rceil$ separately sorted lists.

For sorting and merging, we use nested integer-based Judy arrays. For each batch of input we first fill such a structure – merging duplicate keys as they are encountered – and then traverse it in order, writing a sorted list.

We have found $1.5 \cdot 10^8$ to be a suitable value for K, using about 4.2 GB of memory per list-sorting process. In our development environment we use 10 such processes and produce 160 lists in 130 wall-clock minutes (1233 CPU minutes) for the full data set with full wildcarding.

4.3 Merging and creating the tree

The next step encompasses two subtasks – merging the sorted lists generated into one large sorted list (with duplicate entries merged), and using that large sorted list to generate an indexing tree.

The merging task involves, in our configuration, a P-way merge with $P \approx 160$. We perform this merge using a binary heap for replacement selection in $\log P$ time as outlined in Knuth (1998). Each node in the heap consists of a file handle, one "active" entry (which determines the value of the node), and a read buffer. After being popped from the heap, a node is reinserted if a next entry can be read from the read buffer or the file.

As they emerge in order from the merging section of the program, entries with duplicate keys are merged with their values added.

The tree-building routine receives all the entries to be stored correctly ordered and merged. It proceeds according to the following algorithm:

1. Space is left for the root node at the beginning of the file. We note the offset *after* this space as the "current generation offset". An empty "current node" is created.
2. For each input entry:
   (a) The entry is added as the last entry in the current node.
   (b) If the current node is now full, or if there are no more input entries, it is written to disk and then cleared.
3. We note down the current file offset (as used for writing) as the "next generation offset". We seek back to the current generation offset, and begin reading through the nodes until we reach the next generation offset, obtaining an in-order sequence of all nodes in the current generation

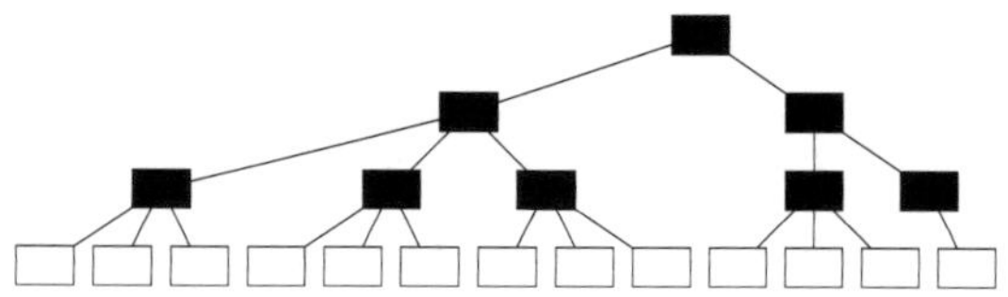

Figure 2: Illustration of the "all but leaves" caching strategy. Filled nodes are kept in memory, unfilled ones are left on disk. The maximal branching factor is 3 here (as compared to 127 in our trees).

(initially all leaf nodes). The sequence is read in lazily.

4. If this sequence is shorter than the number of entries in a node, it is used to construct the root node, which is then written to disk, and the process returns.
5. Otherwise, we repeat the process from the second step, with the following value replacements:
   - The next generation offset becomes the new current generation offset.
   - Each node read in from the file generates a new "input entry", with the key of the first entry of the node as the key, and the file offset pointing to the node as the value.

In our development environment this task currently takes around 283 minutes.

5 Using the indexing structure

5.1 Initialization and caching

The dictionary is loaded into a Judy array in RAM. The unigram counts are loaded into an integer array.

Finally, the upper levels of the trees are loaded into memory to be used as a cache. Since it is possible with only 3.3 GB of RAM, we recommend caching *all* nodes that are not leaves, as seen in Figure 2. Since we use broad trees, the number of leaves we can reach is relatively large compared to the number of internal nodes we need to cache.

5.2 Performing a query

The querying machinery assumes that queries are formulated in terms of integer tokens, and offers an interface to the dictionary so the caller can perform this transformation. This enables the caller to reuse integer mappings over multiple queries, and leaves the querying system loosely coupled to the application-specific preprocessing.

When a query arrives, all the tokens are first mapped to integers (using preprocessing and/or a dictionary). If this process fails for any token, the query returns early with frequency zero.

Otherwise, a conventional B-tree lookup is performed. This entails performing a binary search through the children of each node (with the value of each node considered as the value of its first entry, with entries in leaves identified by keys). In an internal node, after such a search, the node which has been located is loaded (from disk or memory cache) and the process repeats. In a leaf, it is checked whether the match found is *exact*, returning either its associated frequency value or 0 accordingly.

Empirically we have found usage of `lseek(2)` and `read(2)` to be the most performant way to perform the disk reads practically. For threaded applications `mmap(2)` may be more appropriate, as our method would require synchronization.

6 Performance

6.1 Testing setup

The development environment referred to elsewhere, `A`, is a high-performance computer with four eight-core 2.2GHz CPUs, 256 GB of RAM, and a number of 10 000 RPM hard disk drives. We also tested on `B` which is the same system augmented with 500 GB of solid state storage, and `C` which is an off-the-shelf PC with 8 GB of RAM, a 7200 RPM HDD and a single 2.93GHz CPU.

In development and preliminary testing, however, we discovered that the impact of disk caching made straightforward time measurements misleading. As seen in Figure 3, these measurements tended to be drastically affected by accumulation of large parts of the disk structure into cache, and as such showed ever-decreasing query times.

However, we have also observed that the required random disk access (a potentially "far" seek, followed by a read) dominates all other factors in the querying process in terms of cost. Our performance in terms of required random read accesses need not be measured: as noted in Subsection 5.1 we use a caching strategy which makes it self-evident that exactly one read access is required per query. Our

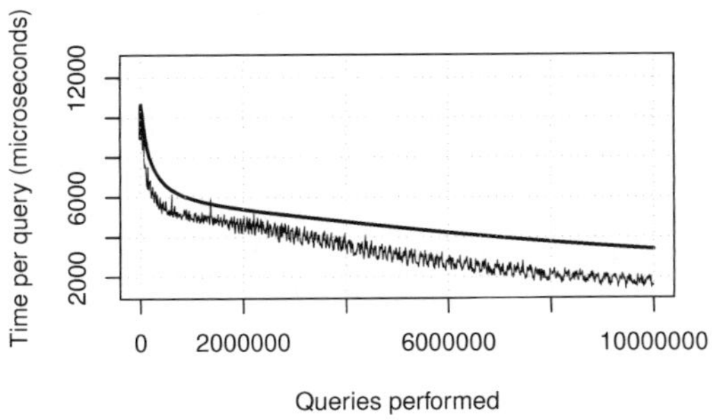

Figure 3: A test run of around 10 000 000 queries in A, illustrating how caching distorts timing information in lengthy tests. The wide line is cumulative average, the narrow one query-time average for the last 1 000 queries. The test run does not reach the stable state of a fully cached file.

	N	μ_R	μ_Q	$\sigma_{\|Q-R\|}$
A	10	6 089.41	6 069.55	260.05
A	100	6 135.54	6 149.60	640.05
A	1 000	6 094.83	6 097.82	477.35
B	10	299.50	313.59	11.09
B	100	298.43	317.14	15.02
B	1 000	308.39	326.00	9.62
C	10	14 763.60	14 924.81	818.90
C	100	14 763.11	14 769.24	634.99
C	1 000	14 776.43	14 708.51	817.47

Table 1: Performance measurements. N is test size, in batches of 100 queries and 100 random node-reads. All measurements in μs. μ_Q is mean time to make a test query. μ_R is mean time to read a random leaf node. $\sigma_{|Q-R|}$ is the sample standard deviation for the *difference* $Q_i - R_i$ between corresponding samples. (By definition, $\mu_{|Q-R|} = \mu_Q - \mu_R$.)

Tree breadth	127
Caching strategy	All but leaves
Total memory use	3.3 GB
Disk accesses per search	1
Leaf size	2 923 bytes
Generation time	431 minutes

Table 2: Vital numbers for our implementation. Generation time is based on adding up the measured wall-clock times reported elsewhere and is of course dependent on our development environment.

performance testing, then, focuses on justifying our assertion that random disk access time is dominant. With this shown, we will have justified random-disk-access-count as a valid way to measure performance, and thus established our chief result.

We generated lists of test queries from the 1T data set with the same distribution as the preprocessed and merged entries in our structure.

6.2 Results

Table 1 shows measurements of time required for queries vs. time required to read a random leaf node (selected from a uniform distribution) without any querying logic. The random-read tests were *interleaved* with the querying tests, alternating batches of 100 queries with batches of 100 random reads. This process was chosen to avoid distorting factors such as differences in fragmentation and size of the area of the disk being read, memory available and used for caching it, as well as variable system load over time.

As can be seen in Table 1, the measurements indicate that time per random read times number of random reads is a very good approximation for time per query. The querying overhead seems to be on the order of 15μs, which is around 5% of the time per node access on the SSD, and less than 0.2% of the access time on the hard drives. It seems justified to measure the performance of our system by random disk access *count*.

We have justified our central assertion that our indexing structure can answer queries using exactly one random disk access per query, as well as the underlying assumption that this is a meaningful way to measure its performance. The performance of our system on any particular hardware can then be estimated from the time the system uses for normal random disk accesses.

In terms of random reads per search, our result is clearly the best *worst-case* result achievable without loading the entire data set into memory: a single disk read (well below the size of a disk sector on a modern disk) per search. Naturally, further improvements could still be made in average-case performance, as well as in achieving equivalent results while using less resources.

The disk space required for the lookup structure

Wildcarding	2	3	4	5	Total
Full	3.6	23	80	221	327
None	3.4	15	24	24	65

Table 3: Disk space, in gigabytes, required for trees with and without wildcarding, by n and in total.

as a whole is summarized in Table 3. The full tree set with full wildcarding requires 327 GB. Wildcarding greatly affects the distribution of the entries: before wildcarding, the 4-grams are in fact more numerous than the 5-grams. Many real applications would not require full wildcarding capabilities.

7 Application adaptation and future work

Our method may be improved in several ways, leaving avenues open for future work.

Firstly and most importantly, it is natural to attempt applying our indexing structure to a real task. The work of Bansal and Klein (2011) has served as a motivating example. Implementing their method with "on-line" lookup would be a natural next step.

For other researchers who wish to use our indexing machinery, it has been made available as free software and may be retrieved at `http://github.com/svk/libltquery`.

If wildcarding is not required, a lowering of storage and memory requirements can be achieved by disabling it. This will reduce storage costs to about 21.52% or around 75 GB (and memory requirements approximately proportionally). Generalizing from this, if only *certain kinds* of wildcarded queries will be performed, similar benefits can be achieved by *certain kinds* of wildcarded (or even non-wildcarded) queries. For instance, less than 40% of the structure would suffice to perform the queries used by Bansal and Klein (2011).

Disk and memory efficiency could be improved by applying compression techniques to the nodes, though this is a balancing act as it would also increase computational load.

Furthermore, performance could be increased by using a layered approach that would be able to resolve *some* queries without accessing the disk at all. This is more feasible for an application where information is available about the approximate distribution of the coming queries.

References

Mohit Bansal and Dan Klein. 2011. Web-scale features for full-scale parsing. In *Proceedings of the 49th Annual Meeting of the Association for Computational Linguistics: Human Language Technologies - Volume 1*, HLT '11, pages 693–702, Stroudsburg, PA, USA. Association for Computational Linguistics.

Doug Baskins. 2004. Judy arrays. `http://judy.sourceforge.net/index.html`. (Online; accessed November 18, 2011).

R. Bayer and E. M. McCreight. 1972. Organization and maintenance of large ordered indexes. *Acta Informatica*, 1:173–189. 10.1007/BF00288683.

Tobias Hawker, Mary Gardiner, and Andrew Bennetts. 2007. Practical queries of a massive n-gram database. In *Proceedings of the Australasian Language Technology Workshop 2007*, pages 40–48, Melbourne, Australia, December.

Donald E. Knuth. 1998. *The Art of Computer Programming, volume 3: Sorting and Searching*. Addison Wesley, second edition.

Dekang Lin, Kenneth Church, Heng Ji, Satoshi Sekine, David Yarowsky, Shane Bergsma, Kailash Patil, Emily Pitler, Rachel Lathbury, Vikram Rao, Kapil Dalwani, and Sushant Narsale. 2010. New tools for web-scale n-grams. In *Proceedings of the Seventh conference on International Language Resources and Evaluation (LREC'10)*, Valletta, Malta, may.

Satoshi Sekine and Kapil Dalwani. 2010. Ngram search engine with patterns combining token, POS, chunk and NE information. In *Proceedings of the Seventh International Conference on Language Resources and Evaluation (LREC'10)*, Valletta, Malta, may.

D. Talbot and M. Osborne. 2007a. Smoothed bloom filter language models: Tera-scale LMs on the cheap. In *Proceedings of the 2007 Joint Conference on Empirical Methods in Natural Language Processing and Computational Natural Language Learning (EMNLP-CoNLL)*, pages 468–476.

David Talbot and Miles Osborne. 2007b. Randomised language modelling for statistical machine translation. In *Proceedings of the 45th Annual Meeting of the Association of Computational Linguistics*, pages 512–519, Prague, Czech Republic, June. Association for Computational Linguistics.

Unified Extraction of Health Condition Descriptions

Ivelina Nikolova
Institute of Information and Communication Technologies
Bulgarian Academy of Sciences
2, Acad. G. Bonchev Str, 1113 Sofia
iva@lml.bas.bg

Abstract

This paper discusses a method for identifying diabetes symptoms and conditions in free text electronic health records in Bulgarian. The main challenge is to automatically recognise phrases and paraphrases for which no "canonical forms" exist in any dictionary. The focus is on extracting blood sugar level and body weight change which are some of the dominant factors when diagnosing diabetes. A combined machine-learning and rule-based approach is applied. The experiment is performed on 2031 sentences of diabetes case history. The F-measure varies between 60 and 96% in the separate processing phases.

1 Introduction

Electronic Health Records (EHRs) are a rich source of information regarding patient's health condition and treatment over time but they often exist as free text only. Currently great efforts are put into structuring such data and making them available for further automatic processing, the so-called *secondary use of EHRs*. Following this line of work in this paper we present a pilot study for extracting condition descriptions from EHRs in Bulgarian with the help of NLP techniques thus making a step toward the structuring of the free text. The specificity of the EHRs as a combination of biomedical terminology in an underresourced language and a source of valuable health-care data makes them attractive for various medical and language research tasks. We present an algorithm which comprises machine learning (ML) techniques and rule-based analysis to automatically identify phrases and paraphrases, for which no "canonical forms" exist in any dictionary, with minimal effort. We analyse anonymous EHRs of patients diagnosed with diabetes.

We focus on extracting the levels of blood sugar and body weight change (examples are given in table 1) which are some of the dominant factors when diagnosing diabetes but we believe this approach can extend to recognise also other symptoms or medication expressions which have similar record structure. We extract information which is on one hand very important for the professionals and on the other hand not directly observable in a collection of unstructured documents because of its composite meaning. In Bulgarian EHRs laboratory data is sometimes present inline in the text only and means for extracting such information from the plain text message are often needed.

The paper is structured as follows: section 2 presents related studies, section 4 describes the method, and section 3 the experiments. The results are given in section 5 and the conclusion in section 6.

2 Related Work

There are several successful systems for identifying patient characteristics and health conditions, mostly in English documents. The one presented by Savova et al. (2008) solves the task of identifying the smoking status of patients by accurately classifying individual sentences from the patient records. They achieve F-measure 85.57. One of the limitations is the lack of negation detection. Similarly to their approach our source documents are decomposed into sentences which are to be classified. The symptom

Proceedings of the NAACL HLT 2012 Student Research Workshop, pages 23–28,
Montréal, Canada, June 3-8, 2012.

descriptions are short and always written within a single sentence, therefore it is important to filter out the irrelevant sentences. We employ ML techniques and rule-based analysis and in addition deal with negation detection.

Harkema et al. (2009) presents an algorithm called ConText, which determines whether clinical conditions mentioned in clinical reports are negated, hypothetical, historical, or experienced by someone other than the patient. The system is entirely rule-based and infers the status of a condition from simple lexical clues occurring in the context of the condition. This algorithm proves successful in processing different clinical report types with F-measure for negation (75-95%), historical (22-84%), hypothetical (86-96%) and experiencer (100%) depending on the report types. Our work rests on a similar idea – we prepare a set of vocabularies which are learned from data and are used for determining the scope of the expressions of interest but we focus on extracting health conditions, their status, values and negation.

Negation is one of the most important features to be recognized in medical texts. There is a work for Bulgarian by Boytcheva (2005) which specifically tackles the negation by the presence of triggering expression as we do too.

Many systems implement isolated condition identification and rarely complete semantic model of all conditions, e.g. MedLEE (Friedman, 1994), MEDSYNDIKATE (Hahn, 2002) etc. identify the status condition and also modifying information like anatomic location, negation, change over time. In Boytcheva et al. (2010) the authors extract from Bulgarian EHRs the status of the patient skin, limbs, and neck with thyroid gland with high accuracy.

3 Experimental Data

Source Data This work is done on free text EHRs of diabetic patients submitted by the Endocrinology Hospital of the Medical University in Sofia. The health conditions are written in the case history which describes the diabetes development, complications, their corresponding treatment, etc. Symptom descriptions are written within a single sentence (sometimes other symptoms are described in the same sentence too) as shown in table 1.

Our training corpus is a subset of anamnesis sentences regarding only symptom descriptions. It is annotated with symptom type on sentence level and with symptom description on token level. These are excerpts from from 100 epicrises. All sentences are marked with class "bs" (blood sugar), "bwc" (body weight change) or another symptom. The sentences that describe more symptoms have more than one label. These data was used for learning the rules and the vocabularies. The experimental/test dataset consists of 2031 anamnesis sentences annotated with symptoms. The documents are manually sentence split and automatically tokenized. To overcome the inflexion and gain a wider coverage of the rules we also use stemmed forms (Nakov, 2010).

Ex. 1. При изследване кръвната захар е била - 14 ммол/л. (*After examination the blood sugar was - 14 mmol/l.*)
Ex. 2. Постъпва по повод на полиурично-полидипсичен синдром, редукция на теглото и кетоацидоза. (*Enters hospital because of polyuria-polydipsia syndrome, weight reduction and ketoacidosis.*)

Table 1: Examples of symptom descriptions.

Vocabularies The algorithm relies on a set of specific vocabularies manually built from the annotated training set. We build a *Focal Term Vocabulary* which contains words and phrases signalling the presence of the health condition description (e.g. "glycemic control", "hypoglycemia" etc.). It is used for defining the condition in *phase 2*. All single words which appear in this vocabulary except for the stop words form the so called *Key Term Vocabulary* used in the *phase 1* classification task.

There are two vocabularies containing border terms: one with rightmost context border expressions (*Right Border Vocabulary*); and one with left border expressions (*Left Border Vocabulary*). These are conjunctions and phrases separating the blood sugar level description from another observation preceding it. Both vocabularies are sorted in descending order by the probability of occurrence associated with each expression as border term.

A *Vocabulary of Negation Expressions* is also compiled as well as a *Vocabulary of Condition Statuses* (e.g. "good", "bad", "increased" etc.).

4 Methodology

We aim at identifying health conditions in the EHR case history. The problem can be broken down into the following subtasks: **Phase 1**: *identify the relevant sentences*; **Phase 2**: *identify the condition and its status*; **Phase 3**: *identify the values related to the symptom of interest* - mmol/l, kg etc.; **Phase 4**: *identify negation*; **Phase 5**: *identify the scope of the description - match left and right border terms*.

Two experiments for accomplishing *phase 1* have been carried out: a rule-based one and ML-based one. In the ML setting we train a binary classification algorithm. We experiment with 3 feature sets: *(i)* all tokens in the corpus; *(ii)* the tokens from *Key Term Vocabulary* and *(iii)* restricted subset of the *Key Term Vocabulary*. In all cases each sentence is considered a document and each document feature vector contains the following boolean values for each feature: *the feature value is true iff the document contains the corresponding token from the feature set, otherwise it is false*. In this setting we use the experimental corpus which we split in folds for training and testing and the vocabularies which are learned from the training corpus.

In the rule-based experiment, we construct lightweight regular expressions that match symptom descriptions in the training set. We model them in context window of up to 5-7 tokens to the left and right of the focal terms depending on the kind of expression. When composing the rules like in figure 1 we introduce new links between tokens which are not subsequent in the training dataset, if the newly created token sequences would be meaningful focal expressions. The black edges are obtained from the training corpus and the dashed grey one is manually added. This approach would not harm any identification procedure because it can match only an existing sequence in the target text therefore we can only benefit from such augmented rules. Moreover these rules are crafted for stemmed text which partially overcomes the morphological agreement problem (Bulgarian is a highly inflective language) thus they have wider coverage on the possible signalling words (see table 2). The sentences matching these rules are passed to *phase 2*.

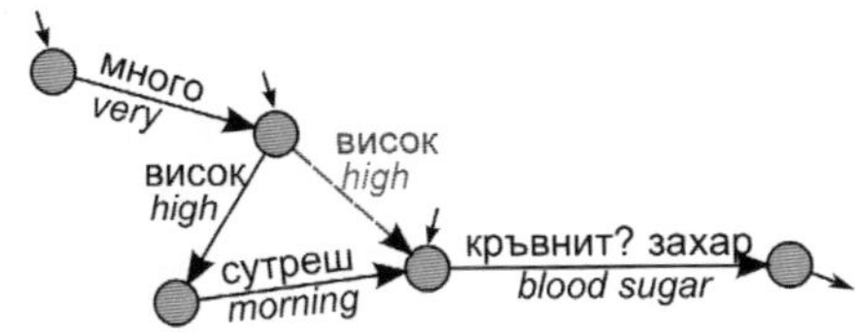

Figure 1: Adding new edges between tokens.

кръвн[аи](т)? захар (*the blood sugar*)
((незадоволителен) OR (добър) OR (лош) OR (отлич)) (гликемич контрол) (*not satisfactory OR good OR bad OR excellent glycemic control*)

Table 2: Phase 1 rules after stemming.

At *phase 2* the condition status is recognised. The blood sugar level is most often cited as *low*, *high* or *normal* and could be also *bad* or *good*, body weight can be *increased* or *decreased*. The context words which signal the status of the condition appear on the left side of the focal terms, such as: с високи стойности на кр. захар (*with high values of the blood sugar*); лош гликемичен контрол (*bad glycemic control*).

Phase 3 analysis is related to the dynamic extension of the right context of the analysed expression in order to cover all necessary attributes. At this phase we aim at identifying the value of the blood sugar test if there is such. The values of this test are given in various ways – as an interval of values; as a maximal value reached during some period or a concrete value. At this step we apply rules matching vocabulary words signalling the type of value representation e.g. между (*between*); до (*up to*); над (*above*); около (*around*).

When the algorithm recognises a word signalling interval value representation such as между (*between*), it takes action to expand the right context to the next two numbers and measuring unit after the second one, but with no more than 7 tokens. If the numbers fall out of this 7-token window they are ignored and the value identification algorithm fails. We determined the 7-token window experimentally by analysing the training set of EHRs where often verbs expressing temporality are connecting/separating the focal terms from the ones describing lab test values (as shown in table 3).

кръвнозахарна стойност до 10-11 ммол/л (*bloodsugar level up to 10-11 mmol/l*)
стойностите на кръвната захар са били (между 4 и 6,5 ммол/л) (*level of the blood sugar has been between 4) (and 6,5 mmol/l*)

Table 3: Recognition of lab test values.

In *phase 4* we recognise negation. We observe only limited occurrences of negations in the text. This is due to the fact that in Bulgarian practice mostly medical conditions with pathological changes are described. The expressions signalling negation appear on the left context of the phrases marked at *phase 1* and they modify the expressions identified at *phase 2*. Some examples are: не съобщава за... (*does not inform about...*); не [много] високи стойности на ... (*not [very] high values of...*).

Phase 5 identifies the symptom description scope. It is determined by the context words which signal the beginning of the expression, its ending and the already identified attributes. The expression of interest either starts at the beginning of the sentence or follows another description and conjunctions. The end of the expression is either coinciding with the end of the sentence, or is signalled by a value of the blood sugar test, or a description of another symptom (see table 4). The border identification rules are applied on the right and on the left of the already identified attributes starting from the rule having highest probability and continue in descending order until a match is found. If no match is found in 7-token context window the right border is considered the right most token of the current expression and the left border of the expression is either the first token of the focal term or negation of the expression or status of the condition.

5 Evaluation

5.1 Phase 1 - Rules vs ML

The evaluation of our approach is performed from several different perspectives. We compare text classification versus rule-based approach at *phase 1*. In the ML setting each input document (meaning each sentence) has a boolean feature vector representing the presence of each token of the feature set in that sentence. The concrete attribute position x_i is *false* if the sentence does not contain the corresponding feature token and is *true* if it contains it.

Beginning of expressions of interest
при кръвна захар... (*with blood sugar...*)
на фона на лош гликемичен контрол... (*on the background of bad glycemic control...*)
с високи стойности на кръвната захар... (*with high values of the blood sugar...*)
Ending of expressions of interest
...кръвна захар - 14 ммол/л. (*...blood sugar - 14 mmol/l.*)
...лош гликемичен контрол и кетоацидоза. (*...bad clycemic control and ketoacidosis.*)

Table 4: Beginning and ending of expressions.

The applied classification algorithm is a standard J48 decision tree which we consider appropriate, given the fact we supply binary data (Visa et al., 2007). We used Weka Data Mining Software (Hall, 2007) for performing the tests. The results with best settings are shown in table 5.

To achieve these results we did several experiments on the test set, using the features selected from the training set. The initial test was done with a feature set comprising all tokens in the text collection except for stop words. The achieved F-measure was about 82 in 10-fold cross-validation, to 89% in isolated experiments and up to 92% on balanced datasets. The precision was as high as 92% and the recall varying from 73 to 85% in the different symptoms. In the second round the feature set contained only tokens from the *Key Term Vocabulary*. This boosted up the classification performance to 90% F-measure for blood sugar and body weight change. When we restricted the feature space once again leaving only the most significant symptom words in the feature space the performance was about 89% F-measure. In all cases the precision varied about 92-94%, and up to 98% when classifying blood sugar level with the full keyword set, which is encouraging. At that time the recall was about 75% in blood sugar identification and this could be explained with the highly imbalanced dataset. Only about 20% of the sentences were blood sugar related and 6% body weight change related. These results

Method %	Precision	Recall	F-measure
J48 bs 22 feat.	94.80	80.00	86.80
J48 bwc 16 feat.	94.30	85.30	89.60
Rule-based bs	96.40	90.00	93.09
Rule-based bwc	98.50	92.00	95.14

Table 5: Level 1 evaluation. ML vs Rule-based best performance.

Phase	Precision	Recall	F-measure
Blood sugar (bc)			
Ph.1 Focus	96.4	90.0	93.09
Ph.2 Status	91	45.5	60.6
Ph.3 Values	88.9	77.8	83
Ph.4 Neg.	96.3	94.2	95.2
Ph.5 Scope	97	96	96.5
Body weight change (bwc)			
Ph.1 Focus	96.6	90.6	93.5
Ph.2 Status	86.2	78.1	82
Ph.3 Values	87.5	70	77.8
Ph.4 Neg.	NA	NA	NA
Ph.5 Scope	82.7	75	78.7

Table 6: Rule performance by level

show that even without introducing domain knowledge and using the full feature space the positive output predictions are reliable. SVM classification was also tested but it was outperformed by J48.

Table 5 shows that the precision of the rule-based approach is higher than the one obtained by automatic classification. However during the error analysis we noticed that in the rule-based setting some true positives were wrongly classified as such because they matched non symptom related expressions in sentences where the symptoms occur and respectively are annotated as positive. In means of precision both approaches differ only in about 2 points which invokes the assumption that they are comparable to each other and could be used as alternatives for experiments on a larger scale even without incorporating domain knowledge, especially in such a task where the accuracy of the extraction is more important than the coverage.

5.2 Phase by Phase Evaluation

Results from the separate phases of rule-based analysis are shown in table 6.

At *phase 2* the tokens available in the training set are completely recognised; there is a group of tokens which are not available in the training set, but during the *phase 1* processing fall into the scope of the expression of interest. These ones are included to the condition description without having assigned any status class. Tokens may not be identified for two reasons – they are not available in the training set or they are misplaced (e.g. the target adjective is following the focal expression instead of preceding it, as it happens in all training set examples). 45% of the attributes expressing blood sugar status are recognised and 78.1% espressing body weight. Although the recall for blood sugar seems to be low at this phase, the result is actually good because during the error analysis we found out that 60% of the tokens which were not identified were equivalent.

At *phase 3* the main problem for value recognition were the alphanumerical expressions of lab test values which occur comparatively rare and have a wide range of spelling variants (and errors). Thus few extraction errors have high influence on the precision. This problem can be easily overcome by pregenerating a list of alphanumeric expressions and their variations. The negation at *phase 4* was recognised with high accuracy.

At *phase 5* all scope problems for blood sugar related expressions are resolved successfully except for one. The interval describing the value of the blood sugar was written as "от 12 ммол/л до 14 ммол/л" *(from 12 mmol/l to 14 mmol/l)* instead of *"from 12 to 14 mmol/l"* like all such examples in the training set. This lead to wrongly recognised right border and only partial recognition of the blood sugar level value. However this issue could be easily overcome by extending the recognition rules with additional "cosmetic" clauses for processing of alphanumeric values as suggested above. It would be helpful for recognition of any symptom to add new lexical alternations and paraphrases in addtion to the stemmed forms in the regex. Our approach is completely driven by the training set analysis because our goal is to see how far do we get on that base.

The extension of the rules as shown on figure 1 helped identifying blood sugar descriptions twice. We believe that such extensions in feature will have higher impact on a larger scale experiment.

6 Conclusion and Future Work

We proposed a unified approach to the recognition of medical descriptions with composite meaning, which are represented by a wide range of paraphrases in the free EHR texts in Bulgarian. The results show a relatively high precision in identifying health condition descriptions in the EHR texts. This was achieved with the use of shallow rules and minor additional effort to extend the rules coverage - stemming of the source documents and adding new meaningful links to the rules where possible. The sentence identification task has nearly the same accuracy in terms of precision when performed with a binary J48 classifier and with the rule-based *phase 1* analysis even without incorporating key terms in the classification. These results give an insight into the possibilities of a further usage of automatic classification for such tasks, due to its flexibility.

As a follow up to this study we will try to generalise this algorithm to a more abstract level so that it can be transferable for the identification of other health conditions, medication etc. We will also put effort in the automatic extraction of symptom identification rules by analysing the classification predictions and the corresponding document feature vectors.

Acknowledgments

The research work presented in this paper is partly supported by grant DO 02-292/December 2008 "Effective search of conceptual information with applications in medical informatics", funded by the Bulgarian National Science Fund in 2009-2012 (EVTIMA).

References

Boytcheva, S., A. Strupchanska, E. Paskaleva, D. Tcharaktchiev, 2005. *Some Aspects of Negation Processing in Electronic Health Records.* In Proc. Int. Workshop LSI in the Balkan Countries, 2005, Borovets, Bulgaria, pp. 1-8.

Boytcheva S., I. Nikolova, E. Paskaleva, G. Angelova, D. Tcharaktchiev and N. Dimitrova, 2010. *Obtaining Status Descriptions via Automatic Analysis of Hospital Patient Records.* Informatica, 34(3):269-278.

Chapman, W., W. Bridewell, P. Hanbury, G. Cooper and B. Buchanan, 2001. *A simple Algorithm for Identifying Negated Findings and Diseases in Discharge Summaries.* J Biomed Inf, 34(5):301-310.

Chapman D. Chu, J.N. Dowling and W.W. Chapman, 2006. *Evaluating the Effectiveness of Four Contextual Features in Classifying Annotated Clinical Conditions in Emergency Department Reports.* AMIA Annu Symp Proc, pp. 141-145.

Elkin, P.L., S.H. Brown, B.A. Bauer, C.S. Husser, W. Carruth and L.R. Bergstrom, et al., 2005. *A Controlled Trial of Automated Classification of Negation From Clinical Notes.* BMC Med Inform Decis Mak, 2005, 5(1), p. 13.

Friedman, C., P.O. Alderson, J.H. Austin, J.J. Cimino and S.B. Johnson, 1994. *A General Natural-Language Text Processor for Clinical Radiology.* JAMIA, 1994 Mar-Apr, 1(2), pp. 161-74.

Hall, M., E. Frank, G. Holmes, B. Pfahringer, P. Reutemann, I. H. Witten, 2009. *The WEKA Data Mining Software: An Update*; SIGKDD Explorations, 11(1).

Harkema, H., J. Dowling, T. Thornblade, W. Chapman, 2009. *ConText: An Algorithm for Determining Negation, Experiencer, and Temporal Status from Clinical Reports.* J Biomed Inf, 2009, 42(5), pp. 839-51.

Hahn, U., M. Romacker and S. Schulz, 2002. *MEDSYNDIKATE - a Natural Language System for the Extraction of Medical Information from Findings Reports.* Int J Med Inf, 2002, 67(1-3), pp. 63-74.

Huang, Y. and H.J. Lowe, *A Novel Hybrid Approach to Automated Negation Detection in Clinical Radiology Reports.* JAMIA, 2007, 14(3), pp. 304-11.

Mutalik, P., A. Deshpande, P. Nadkarni, *Use of General-purpose Negation Detection to Augment Concept Indexing of Medical Documents: a Quantitative Study using the UMLS.* JAMIA, 2001, 8(6), pp. 598-609.

Nakov, P., 2003. *BulStem: Design and Evaluation of Inflectional Stemmer for Bulgarian.* In Proc. of Workshop on Balkan Language Resources and Tools (1st Balkan Conference in Informatics), Thessaloniki, Greece, November, 2003.

Savova G., P. Ogren, P. Duffy, J. Buntrock, C. Chute, 2008. *Mayo Clinic NLP System for Patient Smoking Status Identification* JAMIA, 2008, 15(1), pp. 25-28.

Visa, S., A. Ralescu, M. Ionescu, 2007. Investigating Learning Methods for Binary Data In Proc. Fuzzy Information Processing Society, 2007. NAFIPS '07. Annual Meeting of the North American June 2007, pp. 441-445

Project EVTIMA – "Effective search of conceptual information with applications in medical informatics", `http://www.lml.bas.bg/evtima`

Choosing an Evaluation Metric for Parser Design

Woodley Packard

sweaglesw@sweaglesw.org

Abstract

This paper seeks to quantitatively evaluate the degree to which a number of popular metrics provide overlapping information to parser designers. Two routine tasks are considered: optimizing a machine learning regularization parameter and selecting an optimal machine learning feature set. The main result is that the choice of evaluation metric used to optimize these problems (with one exception among popular metrics) has little effect on the solution to the optimization.

1 Introduction

The question of how best to evaluate the performance of a parser has received considerable attention. Numerous metrics have been proposed, and their relative merits have been debated. In this paper, we seek to quantitatively evaluate the degree to which a number of popular metrics provide overlapping information for two concrete subtasks of the parser design problem.

The motivation for this study was to confirm our suspicion that parsing models that performed well under one metric were likely to perform well under other metrics, thereby validating the widespread practice of using just a single metric when conducting research on improving parser performance. Our results are cautiously optimistic on this front.[1]

We use the problem of selecting the best performer from a large space of varied but related parse disambiguation models ("parsers" henceforth) as the setting for our study. The parsers are all conditional log-linear disambiguators with quadratic regularization, coupled to the English Resource Grammar (ERG) (Flickinger, 2000), a broad-coverage HPSG-based hand-built grammar of English. Analyses from the ERG consist of a syntax tree together with an underspecified logical formula called an MRS (Copestake et al., 2005).

The parsers differ from each other along two dimensions: the feature templates employed, and the degree of regularization used. There are 57 different sets of traditional and novel feature templates collecting a variety of syntactic and semantic data about candidate ERG analyses. For each set of feature templates, parsers were trained with 41 different values for the quadratic regularization parameter, for a total of 2337 different parsers.

The WeScience Treebank of about 9100 sentences (Ytrestøl et al., 2009) was used both for training and testing the parsers, with 10-fold cross validation.

We break down the problem of selecting the best parser into two tasks. The first task is to identify the optimal value for the regularization parameter for each set of feature templates. The second task is to compare the different sets of feature templates to each other, considering only the optimal value of the regularization parameter for each, and select the overall best. We attack each task with each of 14 metrics, and discuss the results.

2 Prior Work

Comparisons of parser metrics have been undertaken in the past. Carroll et al (1998) describe a

[1]Note that we are not suggesting that these metrics provide redundant information for other uses, e.g. predicting utility for any particular downstream task.

Proceedings of the NAACL HLT 2012 Student Research Workshop, pages 29–34,
Montréal, Canada, June 3-8, 2012.

broad range of parser evaluation metrics, and comment on their advantages and disadvantages, but do not offer a quantitative comparison. A number of papers such as Clark and Curran (2007) have explored the difficulty of parser comparison across different underlying formalisms.

Crouch et al (2002) compare two variant dependency-based metrics in some detail on a single LFG-based parsing model, concluding that despite some differences in the metrics' strategies, they offer similar views on the performance of their parser.

The literature specifically seeking to quantitatively compare a broad range of metrics across a large array of parsers is small. Emms (2008) describes the *tree-distance* metric and compares the rankings induced by several variants of that metric and PARSEVAL on a collection of six statistical parsers, finding broad compatibility, but observing frequent disagreement about the relative ranks of two parsers whose scores were only marginally different.

3 Metrics

In our setup, the overall score a metric assigns to a parser is the average of the scores awarded for the parser's analyses of each sentence in the treebank (termed *macro-averaging*, in contrast to *micro-averaging* which is also common). For sentences where the parser selects several candidate analyses as tied best analyses, the actual metric score used is the average value of the metric applied to the different tied best analyses. Fourteen metrics are considered:

- Exact Tree Match (ETM) (Toutanova et al., 2005) - 100% if the returned tree is identical to the gold tree, and 0% otherwise.
- Exact MRS Match (EMM) - 100% if the returned MRS is equivalent to the gold MRS, and 0% otherwise.
- Average Crossing Brackets (AXB) - the number of brackets (constituents) in the returned tree that overlap incompatibly with some bracket in the gold tree. Sign-inverted for comparability to the other metrics.
- Zero Crossing Brackets (ZXB) - 100% if the AXB score is 0, and 0% otherwise.
- Labeled PARSEVAL (LP) (Abney et al., 1991) - the harmonic mean (F_1) of the precision and recall for comparing the set of labeled brackets in the returned tree with the set of labeled brackets in the gold tree. Labels are rule names.
- Unlabeled PARSEVAL (UP) - identical to LP, except ignoring the labels on the brackets.
- Labeled Syntactic Dependencies (LSD) (Buchholz and Marsi, 2006) - the F_1 for comparing the sets of directed bilexical syntactic dependencies extracted from the returned and gold trees, labeled by the rule name that joins the dependent to the dependee.
- Unlabeled Syntactic Dependencies (USD) - identical to LSD, except ignoring the labels.
- Labeled Elementary Dependencies (LED) - the F_1 for comparing the sets of elementary dependency triples (Oepen and Lønning, 2006) extracted from the returned and gold MRS. These annotations are similar in spirit to those used in the PARC 700 Dependency Bank (King et al., 2003) and other semantic dependency evaluation schemes.
- Unlabeled Elementary Dependencies (UED) - identical to LED, except ignoring all labeling information other than the input positions involved.
- Leaf Ancestor (LA) (Sampson and Babarczy, 2003) - the average of the edit distances between the paths through the returned and gold trees from root to each leaf.
- Lexeme Name Match (LNM) - the percentage of input words parsed with the gold lexeme[2].
- Part-of-Speech Match (POS) - the percentage of input words parsed with the gold part of speech.
- Node Count Match (NCM) - 100% if the gold and returned trees have exactly the same number of nodes, and 0% otherwise.

[2]In the ERG, lexemes are detailed descriptions of the syntactic and semantic properties of individual words. There can be multiple candidate lexemes for each word with the same part of speech.

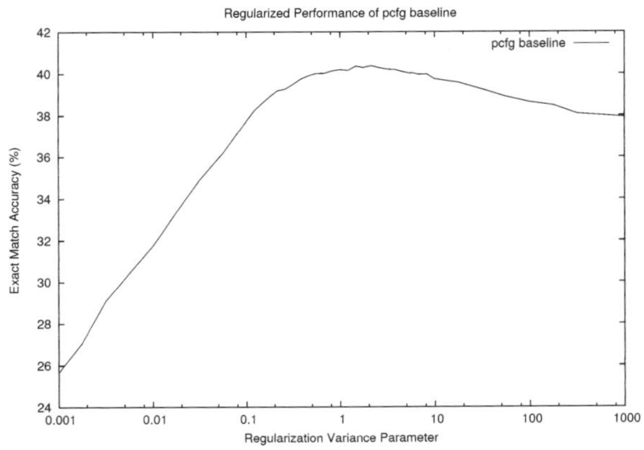

Figure 1: ETM for "pcfg baseline"

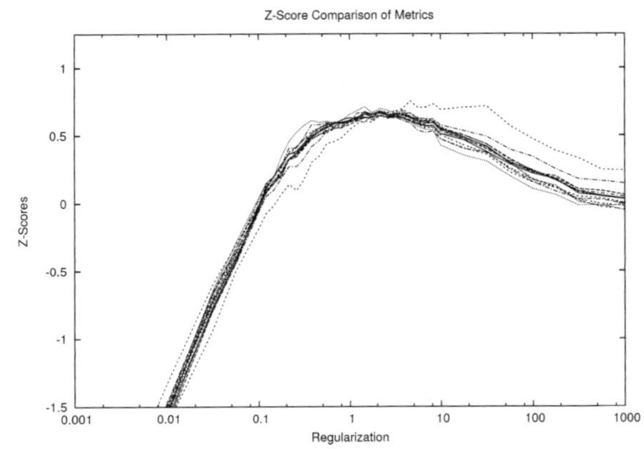

Figure 2: Z-scores for all metrics for "pcfg baseline"

Note that the last three metrics are not commonly used in parser evaluation, and we have no reason to expect them to be particularly informative. They were included for variety – in a sense serving as controls, to see how informative a very unsophisticated metric can be.

4 Optimizing the Regularization Parameter

The first half of our problem is: given a set of feature templates T, determine the optimal value for the regularization parameter λ. We interpret the word "optimal" relative to each of our 14 metrics. This is quite straightforward: to optimize relative to metric μ, we simply evaluate $\mu(M(T, \lambda))$ for each value of λ, where $M(T, \lambda)$ is a parser trained using feature templates T and regularization parameter λ, and declare the value of λ yielding the greatest value of μ the winner. Figure 1 shows values of the ETM as a function of the regularization parameter λ for $T =$ "pcfg baseline"[3]; as can easily be seen, the optimal value is approximately $\hat{\lambda}_\mu = 2$.

We are interested in how $\hat{\lambda}_\mu$ varies with different choices of μ. Figure 2 shows all 14 metrics as functions of λ for the same $T =$ "pcfg baseline." The actual scores from the metrics vary broadly, so the vertical axes of the superimposed plots have been rescaled to allow for easier comparison.

A priori we might expect the optimal $\hat{\lambda}_\mu$ to be quite different for different μ, but this does not turn out to be the case. The curves for all of the metrics peak in roughly the same place, with one noticeable outlier (AXB). The actual peak[4] regularization parameters for the 14 metrics were all in the range $[1.8, 3.9]$ except for the outlier AXB, which was 14.8.

Relative to the range under consideration, the optimal regularization parameters can be seen by inspection to depend very little on the metric. Near the optima, the graphs are all quite flat, and we calculated that by choosing the optimal regularization parameter according to any of the metrics (with the exception of the outlier AXB), the maximum increase in error rate visible through the other metrics was 1.6%. If we ignore LNM, POS and NCM (the nonstandard metrics we included for variety) in addition to AXB, the maximum increase in error rate resulting from using an alternate metric to optimize the regularization parameter drops to 0.41%.

"pcfg baseline" is just one of 57 sets of feature templates. However, the situation is essentially the same with each of the remaining 56. The average maximum error rate increase observed across all of the sets of feature templates when optimizing on any metric (including AXB, LNM, POS and NCM) was 2.54%; on the worst single set of feature templates it was 6.7%. Excluding AXB, the average maximum error rate increase was 1.7%. Additionally exclud-

[3]Note that we are not actually considering a PCFG here; instead we are looking at a conditional log-linear model whose features are shaped like PCFG configurations.

[4]Due to noisiness near the tops of the graphs, the reported optimum regularization parameters are actually the averages of the best 3 values. We attribute the noise to the limited size of our corpus.

ing LNM, POS and NCM it was 0.81%.

Given the size of the evaluation corpus we are using, the significance of an error rate increase of 0.81% is very marginal. We conclude that, at least in circumstances similar to ours, the choice of metric used to optimize regularization parameters is not important, provided we avoid AXB and the variety metrics LNM, POS and NCM.

5 Choosing a Set of Feature Templates

The second half of our problem is: given a collection $\mathcal{T}$ of different sets of feature templates, select the optimal performer. Again, we interpret the word "optimal" relative to each of our 14 metrics, and the selection is straightforward: given a metric μ, we first form a set of parsers $P = \{M(T, \arg\max_\lambda \mu(M(T,\lambda))) : T \in \mathcal{T}\}$ and then select $\arg\max_{p \in P} \mu(p)$. That is, we train parsers using the μ-optimal regularization parameter for each $T \in \mathcal{T}$, and then select the μ-optimal parser from that set.

In our experiments, all 14 of the metrics ranked the same set of feature templates as best.

It is also interesting to inspect the order that each metric imposes on P. There was some disagreement between the metrics about this order. We computed pairwise Spearman rank correlations coefficients[5] for the different metrics. As with the task of choosing a regularization parameter, the metrics AXB, LNM, POS and NCM were outliers. The average pairwise Spearman rank correlation excluding these metrics was 0.859 and the minimum was 0.761.

An alternate method of quantifying the degree of agreement is described below.

5.1 Epsila

Consider two metrics $\mu : P \mapsto \mathbb{R}$ and $\rho : P \mapsto \mathbb{R}$. Assume for simplicity that for both μ and ρ, larger values are better and 100 is perfect. If $x, y \in P$ then the *error rate reduction* from y to x under μ is $\mu^*(x,y) = \frac{\mu(x)-\mu(y)}{100-\mu(y)}$. Let $\epsilon_{\mu,\rho}$ be the smallest number such that $\forall x, y \in P : \mu^*(x,y) > \epsilon_{\mu,\rho} \Rightarrow \rho^*(x,y) > 0$. Informally, this says for all pairs of parsers x and y, if x is at least $\epsilon_{\mu,\rho}$ better than y when evaluated under μ, then we are guaranteed that x is at least a tiny bit better than y when evaluated under ρ. For an unrestricted domain of parsers, we are not guaranteed that such epsila exist or are small enough to be interesting. However, since our P is finite, we can find an ϵ that will provide the required property at least within P.

$\epsilon_{\mu,\rho}$ serves as a measure of how similar μ and ρ are: if $\epsilon_{\mu,\rho}$ is small, then small improvements seen under μ will be visible as improvements under ρ, whereas if $\epsilon_{\mu,\rho}$ is large, then small improvements seen under μ may in fact be regressions when evaluating with ρ.

We computed pairwise epsila for our 14 metrics. A large portion of pairwise epsila were around 5%, with some being considerably smaller or larger.

5.2 Clustering

In order to make sense of the idea that these epsila provide a similarity measure, we applied Quality Threshold clustering (Heyer et al., 1999) to discover maximal clusters of metrics within which all pairwise epsila are smaller than a given threshold. Small thresholds produce many small clusters, while larger thresholds produce fewer, larger clusters.

At a 1% threshold, almost all of the metrics form singleton clusters; that is, a 1% error rate reduction on any given metric is generally not enough to guarantee that any other metrics will see any error reduction at all. The exceptions were that {ETM, EMM} formed a cluster, and {UED, LED} formed a cluster.

Increasing the threshold to 3%, a new cluster {USD, LSD} forms (indicating that a 3% error rate reduction in USD always is visible as some level of error rate reduction in LSD, and vice versa), and ZXB joins the {ETM, EMM} cluster.

By the time we reach a 5% threshold, the majority (7 out of 11) of the "standard" parser evaluation metrics have merged into a single cluster, consisting of {ETM, EMM, ZXB, LA, LSD, UED, LED}. The PARSEVAL metrics form a cluster of their own {UP, LP}.

Increasing the threshold even more to 10% causes 10 out of 11 "standard" evaluation metrics to cluster together; the only holdout is AXB (average number of crossing brackets), which does not join the cluster

[5] The Spearman rank correlation coefficient of two metrics is defined as the Pearson correlation coefficient of the ranks the metrics assign to the elements of P. It takes values between -1 and 1, with larger values indicating higher ranking agreement.

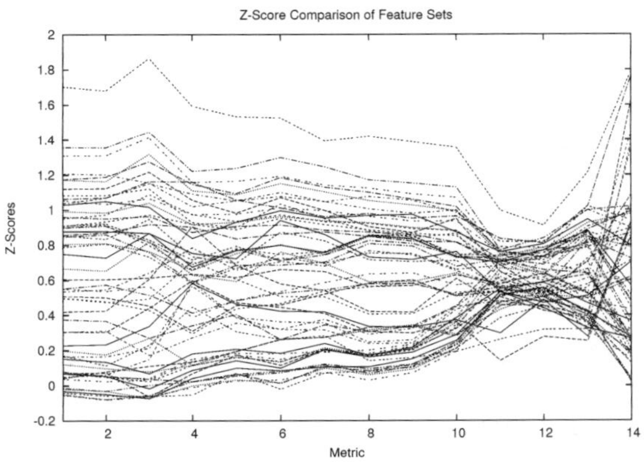

Figure 3: Z-scores for all feature sets on the Y axis (one line per feature set); different metrics on the X axis. The "control" metrics and the outlier AXB are on the far right end.

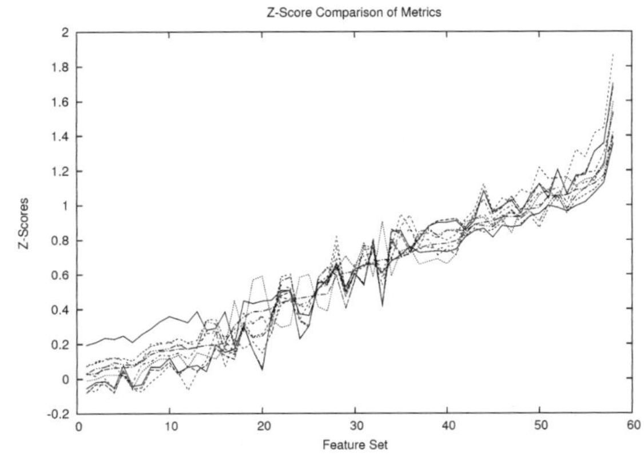

Figure 4: Z-scores for all metrics except AXB, LNM, POS and NCM on the Y axis (one line per metric); different feature sets on the X axis.

even at a 20% threshold.

5.3 Visualization

To qualitatively illustrate the degree of variation in scores attributable to differences in metric as opposed to differences in feature sets, and the extent of the metrics' agreements in ranking the feature sets, we plotted linearly rescaled scores from the metrics (at their optimum regularization parameter value) in two ways.

In Figure 3, the scores of each feature set are plotted as a function of which metric is being used. To the extent that the lines are horizontal, the metrics provide identical information. To the extent that the lines do not cross, the metrics agree about the relative ordering of the feature sets. Note that the three control metrics and the outlier metric AXB are plotted on the far right of the figure, and show significantly more line crossings.

In Figure 4, the score from each metric is plotted as a function of which feature set is being evaluated, sorted in increasing order of the LP metric. As can be seen, the increasing trend of the LP metric is clearly mirrored in all the other metrics graphed, although there is a degree of variability.

6 Conclusions

From both subtasks, we saw that the Average Crossing Brackets metric (AXB) is a serious outlier. We cannot say whether it provides complementary information or actually misleading information; indeed, that might depend on the nature of the downstream application.

We can say with confidence that for the subtask of optimizing a regularization parameter, there is very little difference between the popular metrics {ETM, EMM, ZXB, LA, LP, UP, LSD, USD, LED, UED}.

For the subtask of choosing the optimal set of feature templates, there was even greater agreement: all 14 metrics arrived at the same result. Although they did not impose the exact same rankings, the rankings were similar. It is interesting (and entertaining) that even the three "control" metrics (LNM, POS and NCM) selected the same optimal feature set. It is particularly surprising that even the absurdly simple NCM metric, which does nothing but check whether two trees have the same number of nodes, irrespective of their structure or labels, when averaged over thousands of items, can identify the best feature set.

Our findings agree with (Crouch et al., 2002)'s suggestion that different metrics can offer similar views on error rate reduction.

Clustering based on epsila at the 5% and 10% thresholds showed interesting insights as well. We demonstrated that a 5% error rate reduction as seen on any of {ETM, EMM, ZXB, LA, LSD, UED, LED} is also visible from the others (although the popular PARSEVAL metrics were outliers at this threshold). This has the encouraging implication that a decision made on the basis of strong evidence from just one metric is not likely to be contradicted by evaluations by other metrics. However, we must point out that the precise values of these thresholds are dependent on our setup. They would likely be larger if a significantly larger number of parsers or a significantly more varied group of parsers were considered, and conversely would perhaps be smaller if a larger evaluation corpus were used (reducing the noise).

Our data only directly apply to the tasks of selecting the value of the regularization parameter and selecting feature templates for a conditional log-likelihood model for parsing with the ERG. However, we expect the results to generalize at least to similar tasks with other precision grammars, and probably treebank-derived parsers as well. Exploration of how well these results hold for other tasks and for other types of parsers is an excellent subject for future research.

References

S. Abney, D. Flickinger, C. Gdaniec, C. Grishman, P. Harrison, D. Hindle, R. Ingria, F. Jelinek, J. Klavans, M. Liberman, et al. 1991. Procedure for quantitatively comparing the syntactic coverage of English grammars. In *Proceedings of the workshop on Speech and Natural Language*, pages 306–311. Association for Computational Linguistics.

Sabine Buchholz and Erwin Marsi. 2006. Conll-x shared task on multilingual dependency parsing. In *Proceedings of the Tenth Conference on Computational Natural Language Learning (CoNLL-X)*, pages 149–164, New York City, June. Association for Computational Linguistics.

J. Carroll, T. Briscoe, and A. Sanfilippo. 1998. Parser evaluation: a survey and a new proposal. In *Proceedings of the 1st International Conference on Language Resources and Evaluation*, pages 447–454.

S. Clark and J. Curran. 2007. Formalism-independent parser evaluation with CCG and DepBank. In *Annual Meeting-Association for Computational Linguistics*, volume 45, page 248.

A. Copestake, D. Flickinger, C. Pollard, and I.A. Sag. 2005. Minimal recursion semantics: An introduction. *Research on Language & Computation*, 3(4):281–332.

R. Crouch, R.M. Kaplan, T.H. King, and S. Riezler. 2002. A comparison of evaluation metrics for a broad-coverage stochastic parser. In *Beyond PARSEVAL workshop at 3rd Int. Conference on Language Resources an Evaluation (LREC 2002)*.

Martin Emms. 2008. Tree distance and some other variants of evalb. In Bente Maegaard Joseph Mariani Jan Odjik Stelios Piperidis Daniel Tapias Nicoletta Calzolari (Conference Chair), Khalid Choukri, editor, *Proceedings of the Sixth International Conference on Language Resources and Evaluation (LREC'08)*, Marrakech, Morocco, may. European Language Resources Association (ELRA). http://www.lrec-conf.org/proceedings/lrec2008/.

Dan Flickinger. 2000. On building a more efficient grammar by exploiting types. *Natural Language Engineering*, 6(01):15–28.

L.J. Heyer, S. Kruglyak, and S. Yooseph. 1999. Exploring expression data: identification and analysis of coexpressed genes. *Genome research*, 9(11):1106.

T.H. King, R. Crouch, S. Riezler, M. Dalrymple, and R. Kaplan. 2003. The PARC 700 dependency bank. In *Proceedings of the EACL03: 4th International Workshop on Linguistically Interpreted Corpora (LINC-03)*, pages 1–8.

S. Oepen and J.T. Lønning. 2006. Discriminant-based MRS banking. In *Proceedings of the 5th International Conference on Language Resources and Evaluation (LREC 2006)*.

G. Sampson and A. Babarczy. 2003. A test of the leaf-ancestor metric for parse accuracy. *Natural Language Engineering*, 9(04):365–380.

K. Toutanova, C.D. Manning, D. Flickinger, and S. Oepen. 2005. Stochastic HPSG parse disambiguation using the Redwoods corpus. *Research on Language & Computation*, 3(1):83–105.

Gisle Ytrestøl, Dan Flickinger, and Stephan Oepen. 2009. Extracting and Annotating Wikipedia Sub-Domains. Towards a New eScience Community Resource. In *Proceedings of the Seventh International Workshop on Treebanks and Linguistic Theories*, Groningen, The Netherlands.

Domain-Specific Semantic Relatedness From Wikipedia: Can A Course Be Transferred?

Beibei Yang
University of Massachusetts Lowell
Lowell, MA 01854
byang1@cs.uml.edu

Jesse M. Heines
University of Massachusetts Lowell
Lowell, MA 01854
heines@cs.uml.edu

Abstract

Semantic relatedness, or its inverse, semantic distance, measures the degree of closeness between two pieces of text determined by their meaning. Related work typically measures semantics based on a sparse knowledge base such as WordNet[1] or CYC that requires intensive manual efforts to build and maintain. Other work is based on the Brown corpus, or more recently, Wikipedia. Wikipedia-based measures, however, typically do not take into account the rapid growth of that resource, which exponentially increases the time to prepare and query the knowledge base. Furthermore, the generalized knowledge domain may be difficult to adapt to a specific domain. To address these problems, this paper proposes a domain-specific semantic relatedness measure based on part of Wikipedia that analyzes course descriptions to suggest whether a course can be transferred from one institution to another. We show that our results perform well when compared to previous work.

1 Introduction

Many NLP techniques have been adapted to the education field for building systems such as automated scoring, intelligent tutoring, and learner cognition. Few, however, address the identification of transfer course equivalencies. A recent study by the National Association for College Admission Counseling[2] reveals that 1/3 of US college students transfer to another institution. Correspondingly, University of Massachusetts Lowell (UML) accepts hundreds of transfer students every year. Each transfer course must be evaluated for credits by *manually* comparing its course description to courses offered at UML. This process is labor-intensive and highly inefficient. There is a publicly available *course transfer dictionary* which lists course numbers from hundreds of institutions and their equivalent courses at UML, but the data set is sparse, non-uniform, and always out of date. External institutions cancel courses, change course numbers, etc., and such information is virtually impossible to keep up to date in the transfer dictionary. Furthermore, the transfer dictionary does not list course descriptions. From our experience, course descriptions change over the years even when course numbers do not, and this of course affect equivalencies.

This work proposes a domain-specific semantic relatedness measure using Wikipedia that automatically suggests whether two courses from different institutions are equivalent by analyzing their course descriptions. The goal is to assist transfer coordinators by suggesting equivalent courses within a reasonable amount of time on a standard laptop system. Our model is a mapping function: $f : (C_1, C_2) \rightarrow n, n \in [0, 1]$, where C_1 is a Computer Science (CS) course from an external institution, and C_2 is a CS course offered at UML. Output n is the semantic relatedness score, where a bigger value indicates C_1 and C_2 are more related. Each course description is a short text passage:

- C_1: **[Analysis of Algorithms]** Discusses basic methods for designing and analyzing efficient algorithms empha-

[1] http://wordnet.princeton.edu/

[2] Special Report on the Transfer Admission Process: http://www.nacacnet.org/research/research-data/Documents/TransferFactSheet.pdf

Proceedings of the NAACL HLT 2012 Student Research Workshop, pages 35–40,

sizing methods used in practice. Topics include sorting, searching, dynamic programming, greedy algorithms, advanced data structures, graph algorithms (shortest path, spanning trees, tree traversals), matrix operations, string matching, NP completeness.

- C_2: **[Computing III]** Object-oriented programming. Classes, methods, polymorphism, inheritance. Object-oriented design. C++. UNIX. Ethical and social issues.

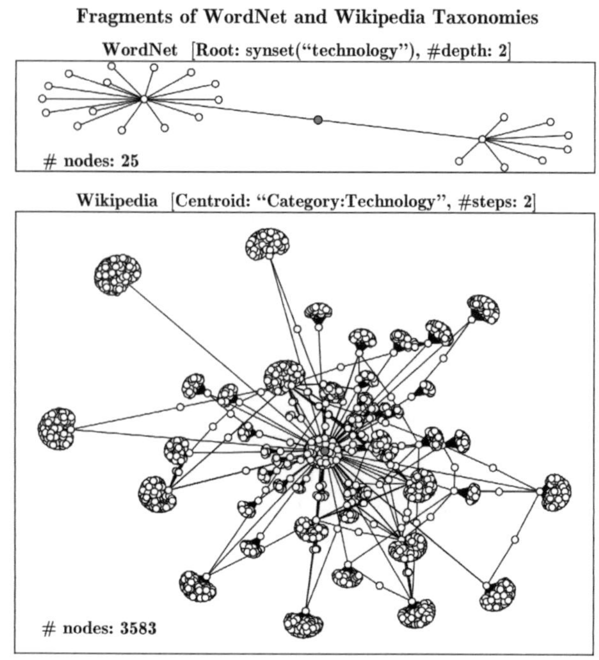

Figure 1. Fragments of WordNet 3.0 (top) and English Wikipedia of 2011/7 (bottom) taxonomies. The root/centroid node is shown in red.

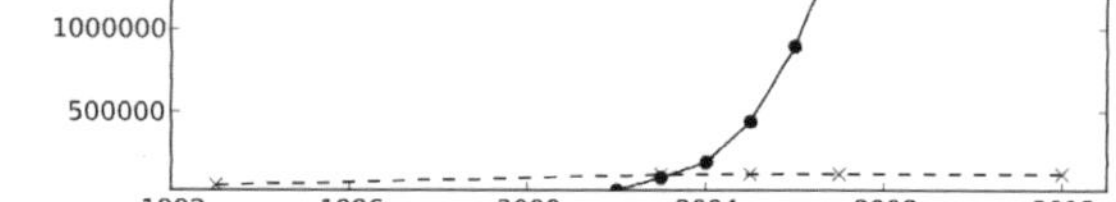

Figure 2. Growth of Wikipedia and WordNet

We choose Wikipedia as the knowledge base due to its rich contents (Figure 1) and continuously coalescent growth (Bounova, 2011). Although Wikipedia was launched 10 years later, it grew much faster than WordNet over the last decade (Figure 2).

The contributions of this paper are twofold. First, we address the problem of domain-specific semantic relatedness using Wikipedia. We propose a method to suggest course equivalencies by computing semantic relatedness among Computer Science course descriptions. Our approach can be easily modified for other majors and even other languages. Second, we evaluate the correlation of our approach and a human judgment data set we built. Both accuracy and correlation indicate that our approach outperforms previous work.

2 Related Research

Semantic relatedness has been used in applications such as word sense disambiguation, named entity disambiguation, text summarization and annotation, lexical selection, automatic spelling correction, and text structure evaluation. WordNet is commonly used as a lexicographic resource to calculate semantic relatedness (Budanitsky and Hirst, 2006). A WordNet-based method uses one or more edge-counting techniques in the WordNet taxonomy (Leacock and Chodorow, 1998; Hirst and St-Onge, 1998). The relatedness of two concept nodes is a function of the minimum number of hops between them.

Some related work calculates co-occurrence on one or more large corpora to deduce semantic relatedness (Sahami and Heilman, 2006; Cilibrasi and Vitanyi, 2007). Two words are likely to be related if they co-occur within similar contexts (Lin, 1998). Others combine lexicographic resources with corpus statistics (Jiang and Conrath, 1997). It has been shown that these composite methods generally outperform lexicographic resource- and corpus- based methods (Budanitsky and Hirst, 2006; Curran, 2004; Mohammad, 2008). Li et al. (2006) propose a hybrid method based on WordNet and the Brown corpus to incorporate semantic similarity between words, semantic similarity between sentences, and word order similarity to measure the overall sentence similarity. Yang and Heines (2011) modify this work to suggest transfer course equivalencies, but the experiment is based on non-technical courses. Due to the WordNet sparsity on technical terms, the experiment does not perform well on Computer Science courses.

In recent years, there has been increasing interest in applying Wikipedia and related resources to question answering (Buscaldi and Rosso, 2006), word sense disambiguation (WSD) (Mihalcea and Csomai, 2007), name entity disambiguation (Ni et al., 2010), ontology evaluation (Yu et al., 2007), semantic web (Wu, 2010), and computing semantic relatedness (Ponzetto and Strube, 2007). Ponzetto and Strube (2007) deduce semantic relatedness of words by modeling relations on the Wikipedia category graph. Gabrilovich and Markovitch (2009) introduce the Explicit Semantic Analysis (ESA) model which calculates TF-IDF (Manning et al., 2008) values for every word in Wikipedia and further uses local linkage information to build a second-level semantic interpreter.

Our approach is different from prior work on Wikipedia. While Mihalcea and Csomai (2007) use the annotation in the page title of a concept to perform WSD, our approach uses a page's parent category as a cue to the correct sense. Ponzetto and Strube (2007) limit their measurement to word pairs, while our work focuses on text of any length. Gabrilovich and Markovitch (2009) computes TF-IDF statistics for every word and every document of Wikipedia which is highly inefficient. They also remove category pages and disambiguation pages. In contrast, our model is mainly based on the category taxonomy and the corpus statistics are limited to metadata that are mostly available in Wikipedia. Furthermore, we compute concept relatedness on a domain-specific hierarchy that weighs both path lengths and diversions from the topic. The domain-specific hierarchy is much smaller than the entire Wikipedia corpus. As a result, our algorithm is more efficient[3] than previous work.

[3]In our experiment, the average time needed to compare one pair of course descriptions ranged from 0.16 second (with partial caching) to 1 minute (without caching) on a 2.6Ghz Quad-Core PC. The most time-consuming part before comparing courses was to index all the Wikipedia tables in a MySQL database, which took overnight (same for ESA). It only took us 15 minutes to go through 19K pages to build a hierarchy of $D = 4$. In contrast, ESA's first level semantic interpreter (which tokenizes every Wikipedia page to compute TF-IDF) took 7 days to build over the same 19K pages. Both implementations were single-threaded, coded in Python, and tested over the English Wikipedia of July 2011.

3 Proposed Method

Our method contains four modules. Section 3.1 explains how to construct a domain-specific hierarchy from Wikipedia. Section 3.2 presents semantic relatedness between concepts. Section 3.3 describes the steps to generate features from course descriptions. And section 3.4 evaluates course relatedness.

3.1 Extract a Lexicographical Hierarchy

When a domain is specified (e.g., CS courses), we start from a generic Wikipedia category in this domain, choose its parent as the root, and use a depth-limited search to recursively traverse each subcategory (including subpages) to build a lexicographical hierarchy with depth D. For example, to find CS course equivalencies, we built a hierarchy using the parent of "Category:Computer science," i.e., "Category:Applied sciences," as the root. The generic category's parent is chosen as the root to make sure the hierarchy not only covers the terms in this domain, but also those in neighbor domains. The hierarchy of "Category:Applied sciences" not only covers Computer Science, but also related fields such as Computational Linguistics and Mathematics.

Both the number of nodes and number of edges in the hierarchy grow exponentially[4] as the depth increases. Therefore, D need not be a big number to cover most terms in the domain. We have found the hierarchy speeds up the semantic measurement dramatically and covers almost all the words in the specific domain. In our experiment on CS courses (D=6), we eliminated over 71% of Wikipedia articles,[5] yet the hierarchy covered over 90% of CS terminologies mentioned in the course descriptions.

3.2 Semantic Relatedness Between Concepts

Similar to the work of Li et al. (2006), the semantic relatedness between two Wikipedia concepts,[6] t_1 and t_2 in the hierarchy is defined as:

$$f'(t_1, t_2) = e^{-\alpha p} \cdot \frac{e^{\beta d} - e^{-\beta d}}{e^{\beta d} + e^{-\beta d}} \quad (\alpha, \beta \in [0, 1]), \quad (1)$$

where p is the shortest path between t_1 and t_2, and d is the depth of the lowest common hypernym of t_1

[4]In the hierarchy we built with "Category:Applied sciences" as the root, the number of edges grows from 177,955 at D=4 to 494,039 at D=5 and 1,848,052 at D=6.

[5]The hierarchy contains 1,534,267 unique articles, as opposed to 5,329,186 articles in Wikipedia.

[6]Each concept corresponds to a Wikipedia page.

and t_2 in the hierarchy (Section 3.1). This is different from related work on semantic relatedness from Wikipedia (Ponzetto and Strube, 2007) in that we not only consider the shortest path (p) between two concepts but also their common distance (d) from the topic, which in turn emphasizes domain awareness.

3.3 Generate Course Description Features

The built-in redirection in Wikipedia is useful for spelling corrections because variations of a term redirect to the same page. To generate features from a course description C, we start by generating n-grams ($n \in [1, 3]$) from C. We then query the *redirection data* to fetch all pages that match any of the n-grams.

The identified pages are still sparse. We therefore query the *title data* to fetch those that match any of the n-grams. Page topics are not discriminated in this step. For example, unigram "Java" returns both "Java (software platform)" and "Java (dance)."

Wikipedia contains a collection of disambiguation pages. Each disambiguation page includes a list of alternative uses of a term. Note that there are two different Wikipedia disambiguation pages: *explicit* and *implicit*. A page is *explicit* when the page title is annotated by Wikipedia as "disambiguation," such as "Oil (disambiguation)." A page is *implicit* when it is *not* so annotated, but points to a category such as "Category:Disambiguation pages," or "Category:All disambiguation pages." We iterate over the pages fetched from the last step, using disambiguation pages to enrich and refine the features of a course description.

Unlike the work of Mihalcea and Csomai (2007) which uses the annotation in the page title of a concept to perform WSD, our approach uses a page's parent category as a cue to the correct sense. Typically, the sense of a concept depends on the senses of other concepts in the context. For example, a paragraph on programming languages and data types ensures that "data" more likely corresponds to a page under "Category:Computer data" than one under "Category:Star Trek."

Algorithm 1 explains the steps to generate features for a course C.

Given the C_1 and C_2 in section 1, their generated features F_1 and F_2 are:

F_1: Shortest path problem, Tree traversal, Spanning tree, Tree, Analysis, List of algorithms, Completeness, Algorithm, Sorting, Data structure, Structure, Design, Data.

F_2: Unix, Social, Ethics, Object-oriented design, Computer programming, C++, Object-oriented programming, Design.

Algorithm 1 Feature Generation (F) for Course C

1. $T_c \leftarrow \emptyset$ (clear terms), $T_a \leftarrow \emptyset$ (ambiguous terms).
2. Generate all possible n-grams ($n \in [1, 3]$) G from C.
3. Fetch the pages whose titles match any of $g \in G$ from Wikipedia *redirection data*. For each page pid of term t, $T_c \leftarrow T_c \cup \{t : pid\}$.
4. Fetch the pages whose titles match any of $g \in G$ from Wikipedia *page title data*. If a disambiguation page, include all the terms this page refers to. If a page pid corresponds to a term t that is not ambiguous, $T_c \leftarrow T_c \cup \{t : pid\}$, else $T_a \leftarrow T_a \cup \{t : pid\}$.
5. For each term $t_a \in T_a$, find the disambiguation that is on average most related (Equation 1) to the set of clear terms. If a page pid of t_a is on average the most related to the terms in T_c, and the relatedness score is above a threshold δ ($\delta \in [0, 1]$), set $T_c \leftarrow T_c \cup \{t_a : pid\}$. If t_a and a clear term are different senses of the same term, keep the one that is more related to all the other clear terms.
6. Return clear terms as features.

Algorithm 2 Semantic Vector SV_1 for F_1 and J

1. **for all** words $t_i \in J$ **do**
2. if $t_i \in F_1$, set $SV_{1i} = 1$ where $SV_{1i} \in SV_1$.
3. if $t_i \notin F_1$, the semantic relatedness between t_i and each term $t_{1j} \in F_1$ is calculated (Equation 1). Set SV_{1i} to the highest score if the score exceeds the preset threshold δ, otherwise $SV_{1i} = 0$.
4. **end for**

3.4 Determine Course Relatedness

Given two course descriptions C_1 and C_2, we use Algorithm 1 to generate features F_1 for C_1, and F_2 for C_2. Next, the two feature lists are joined together into a unique set of terms, namely J. Similar to previous work (Li et al., 2006), semantic vectors SV_1 (Algorithm 2) and SV_2 are computed for F_1 and F_2.

Each value of an entry of SV_1 for features F_1 is reweighed as:

$$SV_{1i} = SV_{1i} \cdot I(t_i) \cdot I(t_j), \quad (2)$$

where SV_{1i} is the semantic relatedness between $t_i \in F_1$ and $t_j \in J$. $I(t_i)$ is the information content of t_i, and $I(t_j)$ is the information content of t_j. Similarly, we reweigh each value for the semantic vector SV_2 of F_2.

The information content $I(t)$ of a term t is a weighed sum of the category information content $I_c(t)$ and the linkage information content $I_l(t)$:

$$I(t) = \gamma \cdot I_c(t) + (1 - \gamma) \cdot I_l(t). \tag{3}$$

Inspired by related work (Seco et al., 2004), the category information content of term t is redefined as a function of its siblings:

$$I_c(t) = 1 - \frac{log(siblings(t) + 1)}{log(N)}, \tag{4}$$

where $siblings(t)$ is the number of siblings for t on average, and N is the total number of terms in the hierarchy (Section 3.1).

The linkage information content is a function of outlinks and inlinks of the page pid that t corresponds to:

$$I_l(t) = 1 - \frac{inlinks(pid)}{MAXIN} \cdot \frac{outlinks(pid)}{MAXOUT}, \tag{5}$$

where $inlinks(pid)$ and $outlinks(pid)$ are the numbers of inlinks and outlinks of a page pid. $MAXIN$ and $MAXOUT$ are the maximum numbers of inlinks and outlinks that a page has in Wikipedia.[7]

Finally, the relatedness of two courses is a cosine coefficient of the two semantic vectors:

$$f(C_1, C_2) = \frac{SV_1 \cdot SV_2}{||SV_1|| \cdot ||SV_2||}. \tag{6}$$

4 Experimental Results

Wikipedia offers its content as database backup dumps (wikidumps) freely available to download. Our application is based on the English wikidump[8] of July 2011. We have extracted redirections, titles, categories, and links from the wikidump into separate tables in MySQL. Using the steps outlined in Section 3.1, we built a table for the hierarchy with "Category:Applied sciences" as the root. The attributes of each table were indexed to speed up queries. Our experiment used $\alpha = 0.2$, $\beta = 0.5$, $\delta = 0.2$, and $\gamma = 0.6$. These values were found empirically to perform well over randomly selected samples.

We randomly selected 25 CS courses from 19 universities that can be transferred to University of Massachusetts Lowell (UML) according to the transfer dictionary. Each transfer course was compared to all 44 CS courses offered at UML, a total of 1,100 comparisons. The result was considered correct for each course if the real equivalent course in UML appears among the top 3 in the list of highest scores. We excluded all Wikipedia pages whose titles contained specific dates or were annotated as "magazine", "journal", or "album." We removed both general and domain stop words (such as "course," "book," and "student") from course descriptions. If a course description contains the keywords "not" or "no," e.g., "This course requires no computer programming skills," the segment after such keyword is ignored.

We tested our approach against the work by Li et al. (2006) and TF-IDF on the same data set of course descriptions. The accuracy of our proposed approach is 72%, compared to 52% using Li et al. (2006), and 32% using TF-IDF.

Algorithm	Pearson's correlation	p-value
Our approach	0.85	$6.6 \cdot 10^{-10}$
Li et al. (2006)	0.57	0.0006
TF-IDF	0.73	$2 \cdot 10^{-6}$

Table 1. Pearson's correlation of course relatedness scores with human judgments.

Since the transfer dictionary is always out of date, we found a few equivalent course pairs that were unintuitive. To make a more meaningful evaluation, we set up a human judgment data set. We gave 6 annotators (CS students and professors) a list of 32 pairs of courses, with only course titles and descriptions. They independently evaluated whether each pair is equivalent on a scale from 1 to 5. We averaged their evaluations for each pair and converted the scale from [1,5] to [0,1]. Next, we ran our approach, the work by Li et al. (2006), and TF-IDF on the same 32 course pairs. Table 1 reports the Pearson's correlation coefficient of course relatedness scores with human judgment, and statistical significances. Our approach has a higher correlation to the human judgment data set compared to previ-

[7]The computation of $MAXIN$ and $MAXOUT$ could be time-consuming. They are therefore based on the entire Wikipedia instead of the constructed hierarchy to avoid the recalculation when the domain changes. This also ensures the maximum linkage information is unbiased for every domain. For the July 2011 wikidump, page "Geographic coordinate system" has the most in-links, a total of 575,277. Page "List of Italian communes (2009)" has the most out-links, a total of 8,103.

[8]http://dumps.wikimedia.org/enwiki/20110722/

ous work. Furthermore, a smaller p-value indicates our approach is more likely to correlate with human judgment.

During the experiment, we have found some misclassified categories in the wikidump.[9] For example, "Category:Software" has over 350 subcategories with names similar to "Category:A-Class Britney Spears articles," or "Category:FA-Class Coca-Cola articles." None of these appears in the Wikipedia website or the Wikipedia API[10] as a subcategory of "Category:Software." More study is required on how they are formed.

5 Conclusion

This paper presents a domain-specific algorithm to suggest equivalent courses based on analyzing their semantic relatedness using Wikipedia. Both accuracy and correlation suggest our approach outperforms previous work. Future work includes comparing our approach with ESA, experimenting on more courses from more universities, and adapting our work to courses in other languages.

Acknowledgments

The authors thank Dr. Karen M. Daniels for reviewing drafts of this paper. We also appreciate the insightful suggestions from Dr. Saif Mohammad at the early stage of our work. Last, but not least, we thank the reviewers for their comments that guided improvement of the contents of this paper.

References

Gergana Bounova. 2011. *Topological Evolution of Networks: Case Studies in the US Airlines and Language Wikipedias*. Ph.D. thesis, MIT.

Alexander Budanitsky and Graeme Hirst. 2006. Evaluating Wordnet-based measures of lexical semantic relatedness. *Computational Linguistics*, 32:13–47.

David Buscaldi and Paolo Rosso. 2006. Mining knowledge from Wikipedia from the question answering task. In *Proc. 5th Int'l. Conf. on Language Resources & Evaluation*, Genoa, Italy.

Rudi L. Cilibrasi and Paul M. B. Vitanyi. 2007. The google similarity distance. *IEEE Trans. on Knowledge & Data Engineering*, 19:370–383.

James R. Curran. 2004. *From Distributional to Semantic Similarity*. Ph.D. thesis, Univ. of Edinburgh.

Evgeniy Gabrilovich and Shaul Markovitch. 2009. Wikipedia-based semantic interpretation for NLP. *J. AI Research*, 34:443–498.

Graeme Hirst and David St-Onge, 1998. *Lexical Chains as Representation of Context for the Detection and Correction Malapropisms*. The MIT Press.

Jay J. Jiang and David W. Conrath. 1997. Semantic similarity based on corpus statistics and lexical taxonomy. In *Proc. Int'l. Conf. on Research in Computational Linguistics*, pages 19–33.

Claudia Leacock and Martin Chodorow. 1998. Using corpus statistics and Wordnet relations for sense identification. *Computational Linguistics*, 24:147–165.

Yuhua Li, David McLean, Zuhair A. Bandar, James D. O'Shea, and Keeley Crockett. 2006. Sentence similarity based on semantic nets and corpus statistics. *IEEE Trans. on Knowledge and Data Engineering*, 18.

Dekang Lin. 1998. Extracting collocations from text corpora. In *Workshop on Computational Terminology*.

Christopher D. Manning, Prabhakar Raghavan, and Hinrich Schütze. 2008. *Introduction to Information Retrieval*. Cambridge University Press.

Rada Mihalcea and Andras Csomai. 2007. Wikify!: linking documents to encyclopedic knowledge. In *Proc. 16th ACM Conf. on Information & Knowledge Management*, pages 233–242.

Saif Mohammad. 2008. *Measuring Semantic Distance Using Distributional Profiles of Concepts*. Ph.D. thesis, Univ. of Toronto, Toronto, Canada.

Yuan Ni, Lei Zhang, Zhaoming Qiu, and Wang Chen. 2010. Enhancing the open-domain classification of named entity using linked open data. In *Proc. 9th Int'l. Conf. on the Semantic Web*, pages 566–581.

Simone Paolo Ponzetto and Michael Strube. 2007. Knowledge derived from Wikipedia for computing semantic relatedness. *J. AI Research*, 30:181–212, October.

Mehran Sahami and Timothy D. Heilman. 2006. A web-based kernel function for measuring the similarity of short text snippets. In *Proc. 15th Int'l. Conf. on WWW*.

Nuno Seco, Tony Veale, and Jer Hayes. 2004. An intrinsic information content metric for semantic similarity in Wordnet. In *Proc. 16th European Conf. on AI*.

Fei Wu. 2010. *Machine Reading: from Wikipedia to the Web*. Ph.D. thesis, Univ. of Washington.

Beibei Yang and Jesse M. Heines. 2011. Using semantic distance to automatically suggest transfer course equivalencies. In *Proc. 6th Workshop on Innovative Use of NLP for Building Educational Applications*, pages 142–151.

Jonathan Yu, James A. Thom, and Audrey Tam. 2007. Ontology evaluation using Wikipedia categories for browsing. In *Proc. 16th ACM Conf. on Information and Knowledge Management*, pages 223–232.

[9] We have analyzed wikidumps of July 2011 and Oct 2010 and the problem persists in both versions.

[10] https://www.mediawiki.org/wiki/API

Using Ontology-based Approaches to Representing Speech Transcripts for Automated Speech Scoring

Miao Chen
School of Information Studies
Syracuse University
Syracuse, NY 13244, USA
mchen14@Syr.edu

Abstract

This paper presents a thesis proposal on approaches to automatically scoring non-native speech from second language tests. Current speech scoring systems assess speech by primarily using acoustic features such as fluency and pronunciation; however content features are barely involved. Motivated by this limitation, the study aims to investigate the use of content features in speech scoring systems. For content features, a central question is how speech content can be represented in appropriate means to facilitate automated speech scoring. The study proposes using ontology-based representation to perform concept level representation on speech transcripts, and furthermore the content features computed from ontology-based representation may facilitate speech scoring. One baseline and two ontology-based representations are compared in experiments. Preliminary results show that ontology-based representation slightly improves performance of one content feature for automated scoring over the baseline system.

1 Introduction

With increasing number of language learners taking second language tests, the resulting responses add a huge burden to testing agencies, and thus automated scoring has become a necessity for efficiency and objectivity. Speaking, an important aspect for assessing second language speakers' proficiency, is selected as the context of the study. The general goal is to investigate new approaches to automatic scoring of second language speech.

When giving a speaking test in computer-mediated environment, test-takers' responses are typically recorded as speech files. These files can be considered to contain two layers: sound and text. The sound is about the acoustic side of speech, whose features have been used to assess speaking proficiency in existing automated speech-scoring systems (Dodigovic, 2009; Zechner et al., 2009). However, the text side, which is about the content of speech, is by far not well addressed in scoring systems, mainly due to the imperfect performance of automatic speech recognizer systems. As content is an integral part of speech, adding content features to existing scoring systems may further enhance system performance, and thus this study aims to examine the use of content features in speech scoring systems.

In order to acquire speech content, speech files need to be transcribed to text files, by human or Automatic Speech Recognition (ASR). The resulted text files, namely, speech transcripts, are to be processed to extract content features. Moreover, representation of text content (e.g. in vectors) is important because it is the pre-requisite for computing content features and building speech scoring models. Therefore this study focuses on representing content of speech transcripts to facilitate automatic scoring of speech.

Speech transcripts can be seen as a special type of text documents, and therefore document representation approaches shed light on representation of speech transcripts, such as Salton et al. (1975),

Proceedings of the NAACL HLT 2012 Student Research Workshop, pages 41–47,
Montréal, Canada, June 3-8, 2012. ©2012 Association for Computational Linguistics

Deerwester et al. (1990), Lewis (1992), Kaski (1997), He et al. (2004), Arguello et al. (2008), Hotho et al. (2003a). On the other hand, written essays, the output of writing section of second language test, share great similarity with speech transcripts, and representation of essays also has implications on speech transcript representation, such as Burstein (2003), Attali & Burstein (2006), and Larkey & Croft (2003).

Existing document representation approaches are primarily statistical and corpus based, using words or latent variables mined from corpus as representation units in the vector. These approaches exhibit two challenges: 1) meaningfulness of representation units. For example, synonymous words represent similar meaning and thus should be grouped as one representation unit. 2) unknown terms. Since words or latent variables in the vector are from training corpus, if an unknown term occurs in the testing corpus then it is difficult to determine the importance of the term in the training corpus because there is no prior knowledge of it in the training corpus.

Ontology concepts, representation units at the concept level, have been less employed in content representation. Hotho et al. (2003a) claim that ontology concepts can help reveal concepts and semantics in documents, and thus we hypothesize ontology-based representation may facilitate obtaining better content features for speech scoring. Ontologies can also complement the abovementioned shortcomings of statistical and corpus based representations by providing meaningful representation units and reasoning power between concepts.

The study compares baseline (statistical and corpus based) and ontology-based approaches. The criterion is representing the same speech transcripts using these approaches, computing content features based on the representations, and comparing performance of content features in predicting speaking proficiency.

2 Related Work

This section reviews work related to representation of speech transcripts, including document representation, essay scoring, and ontology-based representation in text processing.

Document representation has been an important topic in research areas such as natural language processing, information retrieval, and text mining, in which a number of representation approaches have been proposed.

The most common practice of text document representation is the Bag-Of-Words (BOW) approach, illustrated in Salton et al. (1975). The basic idea is that a document can be represented as a vector of words, with each dimension of the vector standing for one single word. Besides using explicit words from documents, latent variables derived from document mining can be used for document representation as well, such as the Latent Semantic Analysis (LSA) and Latent Dirichlet Allocation (LDA) approaches. The representation units are latent concepts or topics and the documents are projected to the semantic space constructed from the latent concepts or topics (Deerwester et al., 1990; Blei, 2012). An important purpose of using the latent variables is to reduce dimensions in document representation and place documents in a more compact space. Some other dimension reduction techniques include Subspace-based methods (Chen et al., 2003) and Self Organizing Map (Kaski 1997; Kaski, et al. 1998).

In the area of automatic essay scoring, essay content are represented to facilitate the scoring. The BOW approach is widely used in essay representation as well, including the e-rater system (Burstein, 2003; Attali & Burstein, 2006) and the experimental system in Larkey & Croft (2003). Representation in the BETSY system (Bayesian Essay Test Scoring System) also involves words, such as frequency of content words, along with specific phrases (Dikli, 2006). The exemplar system employing LSA representation is the Intelligent Essay Assessor system, which performs LSA on training essays and then projects essays to the vector space of latent concepts (Landauer et al., 2003).

Besides representation approaches, content feature computing in essay scoring is useful to content scoring of speech because they share great similarity. Content features can be derived by computing cosine similarity between essay vectors, such as in e-rater (Attali & Burstein, 2006) and Intelligent Essay Assessor (Landauer et al., 2003). The e-rater content feature computing is adopted in this study to compute content features of speech transcripts.

As mentioned in section 1, ontologies can be used to complement the challenges of statistical representation approaches. Ontology concepts have been successfully used in text processing tasks such as text classification and clustering and can help resolve the first challenge, meaningfulness of the representation. Hotho and Bloehdorn along with other people conducted a series of studies in using the ontologies (i.e. WordNet) for text categorization and clustering tasks (Bloehdorn & Hotho, 2004; Hotho et al., 2003a; Hotho et al., 2003b). The goals are to overcome several weaknesses, e.g. synonyms and generalization issues, of the bag-of-words representation by using ontology concept based representation. Basically concepts from ontologies are used as units for text representation and then text processing is performed on top of the ontology-based representation. Explicit Semantic Approach (ESA), proposed by Gabrilovich and Markovitch (2007), is an approach to representing an arbitrary text snippet in vector of Wikipedia concepts for the convenience of further natural language processing. Each Wikipedia concept has text description, which is used to build an invert index to associate words with concepts. The invert index helps represent each word by vector of Wikipedia concepts, and eventually a document can be represented by weighted Wikipedia concepts by adding up the Wikipedia concept vectors of the words that the document contains.

Ontologies can also help resolve the second challenge of statistical representation, the unknown term issue. If a term occurs in the testing corpus but not the training corpus, then the importance of the term can be inferred from external knowledge such as ontologies. The semantic relations defined in ontologies connect relevant concepts and organize them into a tree (i.e. WordNet) or a graph structure (i.e. Wikipedia). Since paths usually exist between two individual concepts, ontologies can support inferences among concepts by using the paths and concept nodes between them. Moreover, semantic similarity between concepts, computed based on ontology knowledge, can be used to infer importance of unknown terms.

WordNet (Fellbaum, 1998) and Wikipedia (Wikipedia, 2012) ontologies are two popular ontologies for computing semantic similarity. A number of similarity approaches have been proposed for similarity calculation according to the different characteristics of the two ontologies (Lin, 1998; Pedersen et al., 2004; Resnik, 1999; Strube & Ponzetto, 2006).

3 Methodology

Experiments are conducted to compare ontology-based representations (experimental systems) and common representations (baseline systems). Two ontology-based methods are employed as the experimental systems, one is about representing transcripts using ontology concepts ("ONTO"), and the other is about inferring weights of unknown terms using ontologies ("OntoReason"). For the baseline, we identify the BOW representation as a common text representation and use it in the baseline system.

3.1 Data Set

The data set comes from an English proficiency test for non-native speakers. For the speaking section, test takers are asked to provide spontaneous speech responses to the prompts[1] (test tasks). There are 4 prompts in the data set, all of which are integrated prompts. An integrated prompt is a test task that first provides test takers some materials to read or listen and then asks them to provide opinions or arguments towards the materials. The responses are then scored holistically by human raters based on a scoring rubric on a scale of 1 to 4, 4 being the highest score. For each score level, the scoring rubric contains guidelines of expected performance on various aspects of speaking ability such as pronunciation, fluency, and content.

The data set contains 1243 speech samples from 327 speakers in total. Manual and automatic methods are used to obtain transcripts of the speech samples. For the manual way, each response is verbatim transcribed by human; and for the automatic way, each response is automatically transcribed by ASR with word error rate of 12.8%. Therefore two sets of transcripts are derived for the speech responses, the human transcripts set and the ASR set.

Since the representation approaches are prompt-specific in the study, meaning vector representations are generated for each prompt, the data set is first split by prompts and then responses are split into training and testing sets within each prompt. Table 1 shows size of the data set and subsets:

[1] Prompts are test tasks assigned to test takers to elicit their speaking responses.

[2] The feature is referred to as "cos.w/6" in Attali and Burstein (2006) because there are usually 6 score levels, while here our

Prompt	Training Set	Test Set	Total
A	143	176	319 (4/79/158/78)
B	140	168	308 (7/86/146/69)
C	139	172	311 (4/74/154/79)
D	137	168	305 (8/75/141/81)

Table 1. Size of data set and subsets. The numbers in parentheses are the number of documents on score levels 1-4.

3.2 Representation Approaches of Speech Transcripts

One baseline approach and two ontology-based approaches are briefly introduced here and implemented in experiments. The approaches are used to generate vectors for computing content features. We also plan to employ other approaches in the future, as described in section 5.

3.2.1 Bag-of-words (baseline)

It takes the view that essays can be represented in vector of words and the value of a word in a vector refers to its weighting on this dimension. It uses the representation method in the e-rater as well, including document-level representation for testing documents and score-level representation for training documents (Attali & Burstein, 2006).

Within each prompt, each testing transcript is converted to a vector (document level representation); training transcripts are grouped by their score levels and for each score level a vector is generated by aggregating all transcripts of this score level (score level representation). We decide to use the tfidf weighting schema with stop words removed after tuning options of the parameters.

3.2.2 Ontology-based Representation (experimental)

ONTO-WordNet approach. Concepts from ontology are identified in speech transcripts and then used to generate concept-level vectors. In practice, concept mapping in transcripts varies according to characteristics of ontologies. The WordNet ontology, containing mostly single words, is used as one case in the study. In the future, we plan to try the Wikipedia ontology, which contains more phrases-based concepts, for ontology-based representation.

Synsets, groups of synonyms, are concepts in WordNet and used as ontology concepts here. Document text is split by whitespace and punctuations to a set of words. Then the words are matched to WordNet synsets. As a word may have multiple senses (synsets), it is necessary to decide which synset to use in WordNet. Therefore we try two sense selection strategies as in Hotho et al.'s (2003a) study: 1) simply use the first sense in WordNet; and 2) do part-of-speech tagging on sentences and find the corresponding sense in WordNet. We find the 1st strategy obtains better performance than the 2nd one and thus decide to use the 1st one. When constructing ontology-based vector, we include both concepts and words in the vector.

3.2.3 Ontology-based Reasoning (experimental)

OntoReason-WordNet approach. This approach is also implemented by using WordNet. First, transcripts are represented by ontology concepts as in section 3.2.2. Then given an unknown concept in test transcripts, we identify its semantically similar concepts (N=5) in the training transcripts and then reason the weight of the unknown concept based on the weights of these similar concepts.

The reasoning makes use of semantic similarity between WordNet synsets. Concept similarity is computed using the edge-based path similarity (Pedersen et al., 2004). We select N=5 concepts from the training transcripts that are most similar to the unknown concept, and compute the weight of the unknown concept in the training transcripts by averaging the weights of the 5 similar concepts.

3.3 Content Feature Computation

The baseline and experimental systems all generate vector representations for speech transcripts. The content features are computed based on vector representation, and all representation approaches employ the same method of computing content features. We choose to use the two content features of the e-rater system, "max.cos" and "cos.w4", as the feature computation method[2] (Attali & Burstein, 2006).

The max.cos feature. This feature identifies which score level of training documents the testing document is closest to. It computes and compares the similarity between the test document and training documents of each score level in vector space, and then makes the score level whose training doc-

[2] The feature is referred to as "cos.w/6" in Attali and Burstein (2006) because there are usually 6 score levels, while here our data has 4 score levels therefore it is written as "cos.w4".

uments are most similar to the test document as the feature value.

The cos.w4 feature. This feature computes content similarity between the test document and the highest level training documents in vector space. Since score 4 is the highest level in our data set of spoken responses, we compute the cosine similarity between the test vector and the score level 4 vector as the feature value.

Given a speech transcript from the test set, we first convert it to a vector using one of the representation approaches, and then compute the max.cos and cos.w4 feature values as its content features.

3.4 Evaluation

Representation approaches are evaluated based on their performance in predicting speaking proficiency of test takers. More specifically, a representation approach generates a vector representation using specific representation units (e.g. words, concepts); for each test transcript, two content features are computed based on the vector representation; Pearson correlation r is computed between each content feature and speaking proficiency to indicate the predictiveness of the content feature resulting from a specific representation. Higher correlation indicates higher predictiveness on speaking proficiency. Lastly, we compare content feature correlations of different representation approaches. We consider that the higher the correlation is, the better the representation approach is.

4 Experiment Results

In the preliminary stage, the BOW (baseline), ONTO-WordNet and OntoReason-WordNet (experimental) approaches are implemented. Meanwhile parameters are optimized to acquire the best parameter setup for each approach. Since the speech files are transcribed by both human and ASR, same experiments are run on both data sets to compare representation performance on different transcriptions. The correlations of the two content features to speaking proficiency are computed for each representation. Tables 2 and 3 show correlations of the max.cos and cos.w4 features respectively:

For the max.cos feature, the average correlation of the ONTO-WordNet approach outperforms the BOW baseline slightly but the correlation drops dramatically when using the OntoReason-WordNet approach, for both the human and ASR transcripts. For the cos.w4 feature, the average correlation of the ONTO-WordNet approach outperforms the BOW, and the OntoReason-WordNet further outperforms the ONTO-WordNet approach, for both the human and ASR transcripts. It shows some evidence that ontology-based representation can improve performance of both content features; the ontology-based reasoning increases performance of the cos.w4 feature but decreases the max.cos feature correlation.

Comparing the performance on human vs. ASR transcripts, the features extracted from the human transcripts exhibit better average correlations than the corresponding features from the ASR transcripts. The results also show that the correlation difference between human and ASR transcripts is moderate. It may indicate that the representation approaches can be employed on ASR transcripts to further automate the speech scoring process.

Prompt	Hum, BOW	Hum, ONTO-WordNet	Hum, Onto-Reason-WordNet	ASR, BOW	ASR, ONTO-WordNet	ASR, Onto-Reason-WordNet
A	0.320	0.333	0.038	0.293	0.286	0.014
B	0.348	0.352	0.350	0.308	0.338	0.339
C	0.366	0.373	0.074	0.396	0.386	0.106
D	0.343	0.323	0.265	0.309	0.309	0.265
Average	0.344	0.345	0.182	0.327	0.330	0.181

Table 2. Correlations between the max.cos feature and speaking proficiency (Hum=using human transcriptions; ASR=using ASR hypotheses).

Prompt	Hum, BOW	Hum, ONTO-WordNet	Hum, Onto-Reason-WordNet	ASR, BOW	ASR, ONTO-WordNet	ASR, Onto-Reason-WordNet
A	0.427	0.429	0.434	0.409	0.416	0.411
B	0.295	0.303	0.327	0.259	0.278	0.292
C	0.352	0.385	0.402	0.338	0.366	0.380
D	0.368	0.385	0.389	0.360	0.379	0.374
Average	0.361	0.376	0.388	0.342	0.360	0.364

Table 3. Correlations between the cos.w4 feature and speaking proficiency (Hum=using human transcriptions; ASR=using ASR hypotheses)

5 Future Work

For future work, we will implement one more baseline (LSA) and two more ontology-based approaches (ONTO-Wikipedia and OntoReason-Wikipedia) and analyze their performance.

Latent semantic analysis (LSA). LSA decomposes a term-by-document matrix generated from training transcripts to three sub-matrices. Then given a test transcript, documents can be projected to the latent semantic space based on the three sub-matrices. The rank k parameter needs to be decided as a parameter for dimensionality reduction purpose by tuning it on the training data.

Using Wikipedia as another case for ontology, two more experimental approaches will be implemented, one for ontology-based representation and the other for ontology-based reasoning.

ONTO-Wikipedia. Wikipedia concepts can be identified in transcripts in two ways: 1) directly find concepts in text window of 5 words; 2) convert a transcript in vectors of Wikipedia concepts using the Explicit Semantic Analysis method, which associates words to Wikipedia concepts and represents arbitrary text using the word-concept associations (Gabrilovich and Markovitch, 2007).

OntoReason-Wikpedia. The concept similarity between Wikipedia concepts is obtained by computing the cosine similarity of the text description of the concepts. The reasoning method of the unknown concept follows the one mentioned in the OntoReason-WordNet approach.

We will compute content features based on these new representations and evaluate the performance according to feature correlations. The current results examine effects of using the WordNet ontology on predicting speaking proficiency, and these new experiments will answer whether the other type of ontology, Wikipedia, has positive effect in speaking proficiency prediction. We will also compare the effects of using different ontologies for ontology-based representations.

The study has implications on effects of different speech transcript representations in predicting speaking proficiency. Since content features are less well explored in automatic speech scoring compared to acoustic features, it also contributes to the understanding of the use and effects of content features in speech scoring.

Acknowledgments

The author would like to than Drs. Klaus Zechner and Jian Qin for their tremendous help and support on the dissertation study.

References

Arguello, J., Elsas, J. L., Callan, J., & Carbonell, J. G. (2008). *Document representation and query expansion models for blog recommendation.* Proceedings of the Second International Conference on Weblogs and Social Media (ICWSM 2008).

Attali, Y., & Burstein, J. (2006). Automated essay scoring with e-rater® V. 2. *The Journal of Technology, Learning and Assessment*, 4(3).

Blei, D. (2012). Introduction to probabilistic topic models. *Communications of the ACM, 77-84.*

Bloehdorn, S., & Hotho, A. (2004). *Boosting for text classification with semantic features.* Workshop on mining for and from the semantic web at the 10th ACM SIGKDD conference on knowledge discovery and data mining (KDD 2004).

Burstein, J. (2003). The E-rater® scoring engine: Automated essay scoring with natural language processing. In M. D. Shermis, Burstein, J.C. (Ed.), *Automated essay scoring: A cross-disciplinary perspective* (pp. 113-121). Mahwah, NJ: Lawrence Erlbaum Associates, Inc.

Chen, L., Tokuda, N., & Nagai, A. (2003). A new differential LSI space-based probabilistic document classifier. *Information Processing Letters*, 88(5), 203-212.

Deerwester, S., Dumais, S. T., Furnas, G. W., Landauer, T. K., & Harshman, R. (1990). Indexing by latent semantic analysis. *Journal of the American Society for information science*, 41(6), 391-407.

Dikli, S. (2006). An overview of automated scoring of essays. *The Journal of Technology, Learning and Assessment*, 5(1).

Dodigovic, M. (2009). *Speech Processing Technology in Second Language Testing*. Proceedings of the Conference on Language & Technology 2009.

Fellbaum, C. (Ed.). (1998). *WordNet: An electronic lexical database*. Cambridge, MA: The MIT press.

Gabrilovich, E., & Markovitch, S. (2007). *Computing semantic relatedness using wikipedia-based explicit semantic analysis*. Proceedings of the 20th International Joint Conference on Artificial Intelligence.

He, X., Cai, D., Liu, H., & Ma, W. Y. (2004). *Locality preserving indexing for document representation*. Proceedings of the 27th Annual International ACM SIGIR Conference.

Hotho, A., Staab, S., & Stumme, G. (2003a). *Ontologies improve text document clustering*. Proceedings of the Third IEEE International Conference on Data Mining (ICDM'03).

Hotho, A., Staab, S., & Stumme, G. (2003b). *Text clustering based on background knowledge* (Technical report, no.425.): Institute of Applied Informatics and Formal Description Methods AIFB, University of Karlsruche.

Kaski, S. (1997). Computationally efficient approximation of a probabilistic model for document representation in the WEBSOM full-text analysis method. *Neural processing letters*, 5(2), 69-81.

Kaski, S., Honkela, T., Lagus, K., & Kohonen, T. (1998). WEBSOM-Self-organizing maps of document collections1. *Neurocomputing*, 21(1-3), 101-117.

Landauer, T. K., Laham, D., & Foltz, P. W. (2003). Automated scoring and annotation of essays with the Intelligent Essay Assessor. In M. D. Shermis, Burstein, J.C. (Ed.), *Automated essay scoring: A cross-disciplinary perspective* (pp. 87–112). Mahwah, NJ: Lawrence Erlbaum Associates, Inc.

Larkey, L. S., & Croft, W. B. (2003). A Text Categorization Approach to Automated Essay Grading. In M. D. Shermis & J. C. Burstein (Eds.), *Automated Essay Scoring: A Cross-discipline Perspective*: Mahwah, NJ, Lawrence Erlbaum.

Lewis, D. D. (1992). *Representation and learning in information retrieval*. (Doctoral dissertation). University of Massachusetts.

Pedersen, T., Patwardhan, S., & Michelizzi, J. (2004). *WordNet:: Similarity: measuring the relatedness of concepts*. Proceedings of the Fifth Annual Meeting of the North American Chapter of the Association for Computational Linguistics (NAACL-04).

Resnik, P. (1999). Semantic similarity in a taxonomy: An information-based measure and its application to problems of ambiguity in natural language. *Journal of Artificial Intelligence*, 11(1999), 95-130.

Salton, G., Wong, A., & Yang, C. S. (1975). A vector space model for automatic indexing. *Communications of the ACM*, 18(11), 613-620.

Strube, M., & Ponzetto, S. P. (2006). *WikiRelated! Computing semantic relatedness using Wikipedia*. Proceedings of the American Association for Artificial Intelligence 2006, Boston, MA.

Wikipedia: The free encyclopedia. (2012, Apr 1). FL: Wikimedia Foundation, Inc. Retrieved Apr 1, 2012, from http://www.wikipedia.org

Zechner, K., Higgins, D., Xi, X., & Williamson, D. M. (2009). Automatic scoring of non-native spontaneous speech in tests of spoken English. *Speech Communication*, 51(10), 883-895.

Deep Unsupervised Feature Learning for Natural Language Processing

Stephan Gouws
MIH Media Lab, Stellenbosch University
Stellenbosch, South Africa
stephan@ml.sun.ac.za

Abstract

Statistical natural language processing (NLP) builds models of language based on statistical features extracted from the input text. We investigate deep learning methods for unsupervised feature learning for NLP tasks. Recent results indicate that features learned using deep learning methods are not a silver bullet and do not always lead to improved results. In this work we hypothesise that this is the result of a disjoint training protocol which results in mismatched word representations and classifiers. We also hypothesise that modelling long-range dependencies in the input and (separately) in the output layers would further improve performance. We suggest methods for overcoming these limitations, which will form part of our final thesis work.

1 Introduction

Natural language processing (NLP) can be seen as building models $h : \mathcal{X} \rightarrow \mathcal{Y}$ for mapping an input encoding $x \in \mathcal{X}$ representing a natural language (NL) fragment, to an output encoding $y \in \mathcal{Y}$ representing some construct or formalism used in the particular NLP task of interest, e.g. part-of-speech (POS) tags, begin-, inside-, outside (BIO) tags for information extraction, semantic role labels, etc.

Since the 90s, the predominant approach has been statistical NLP, where one models the problem as learning a predictive function h for mapping from $h : \mathcal{X} \rightarrow \mathcal{Y}$ using machine learning techniques. Machine learning consists of a hypothesis function which learns this mapping based on latent or explicit features extracted from the input data.

In this framework, h is usually trained in a supervised setting from labelled training pairs $(x_i, y_i) \in \mathcal{X} \times \mathcal{Y}$. Additionally, the discriminant function h typically operates on a transformed representation of the data to a common feature space encoded as a *feature vector* $\phi(x)$, and then learns a mapping from feature space to the output space, $h : \phi(x) \rightarrow y$. In supervised learning, the idea

$\vec{x} \in \mathcal{X}$	**the**	**cat**	**sits**	**on**	**the**	**mat**
$\phi(\vec{x})$	$\phi(x_1)$	$\phi(x_2)$	$\phi(x_3)$	$\phi(x_4)$	$\phi(x_5)$	$\phi(x_6)$
$\vec{y} \in \mathcal{Y}$	B-NP	I-NP	B-VP	O	B-NP	I-NP
NE Tags	**[the cat]$_{NP}$**		**[sits]$_{VP}$**	**[on]$_{O}$**	**[the mat]$_{NP}$**	

Table 1: Example NLP syntactic chunking task for the sentence "the cat sits on the mat". $\mathcal{X}$ represents the words in the input space, $\mathcal{Y}$ represents labels in the output space. $\phi(\vec{x})$ is a feature representation for the input text $\vec{x}$ and the bottom row represents the output named entity tags in a more standard form.

is generally that features represent strong discriminating characteristics of the problem gained through manual engineering and domain-specific insight.

As a concrete example, consider the task of syntactic chunking, also called "shallow parsing", (Gildea and Jurafsky, 2002): Given an input string, e.g.

"the cat sits on the mat",

the chunking problem consists of labelling segments of a sentence with syntactic constituents such as noun or verb phrases (NPs or VPs). Each word is assigned one unique tag often encoded using the BIO encoding[1]. We represent the input text as a vector of words $x_i \in \vec{x}$, and each word's corresponding label is represented by $y_i \in \vec{y}$ (see Table 1). Given a feature generating function $\phi(x_i)$ and a set of labelled training pairs $(x_i, y_i) \in \mathcal{X} \times \mathcal{Y}$, the task then reduces to learning a suitable mapping $h : \phi(\mathcal{X}) \rightarrow \mathcal{Y}$.

Most previous works have focused on manually engineered features and simpler, linear models, including "shallow" model architectures, like the perceptron (Rosenblatt, 1957), linear SVM (Cortes and Vapnik, 1995) and linear-chain conditional random fields (CRFs) (Lafferty, 2001). However, a shallow learning architecture is only as good as its input features. Due to the complex nature of NL, deeper architectures may be re-

[1] E.g. B-NP means "begin NP", I-NP means "inside NP", and O means other/outside.

Proceedings of the NAACL HLT 2012 Student Research Workshop, pages 48–53,
Montréal, Canada, June 3-8, 2012.

quired to learn data representations which contain the appropriate level of information for the task at hand. Prior to 2006, it was computationally infeasible to perform inference in hierarchical ("deep"), non-linear models such as multi-layer perceptrons with more than one hidden layer. However, Hinton (2006) proposed an efficient, layer-wise greedy method for learning the model parameters in these architectures, which spurred a renewed interest in deep learning research.

Still, creating annotated training data is labour-intensive and costly, and manually designing and extracting discriminating features from the data to be used in the learning process is a costly procedure requiring significant levels of domain expertise. Over the last two decades, the growth of available unlabeled data $x \in \mathcal{X}$ and the ubiquity of scalable computing power has shifted research focus to unsupervised approaches for automatically *learning* appropriate feature representations $\phi(x)$ from large collections of unlabeled text.

Several methods have been proposed for unsupervised feature learning, including simple k-means clustering (Lloyd, 1982), Brown clustering (Brown et al., 1992), mutual information (Shannon and Weaver, 1962), principal components analysis (PCA) (Jolliffe, 2002), and independent component analysis (ICA) (Hyvärinen et al., 2001).

However, natural language has complex mappings from text to meaning, arguably involving higher-order correlations between words which these simpler methods struggle to model adequately. Advances in the "deep learning" community allow us to perform efficient unsupervised feature learning in highly complex and high-dimensional input feature spaces, making it an attractive method for learning features in e.g. vision or language (Bengio, 2009).

The standard deep learning approach is to learn lower-dimensional *embeddings* from the raw high-dimensional[2] input space $\mathcal{X}$ to lower dimensional (e.g. 50-dimensional) feature spaces in an unsupervised manner, via repeated, layer-wise, non-linear transformation of the input features, e.g.

$$\hat{y} = f^{(k)}(\cdots f^{(2)}(f^{(1)}(\vec{x}))\cdots),$$

where $f^{(i)}(x)$ is some non-linear function (typically tanh) for which the parameters are learned by back propagating error gradients. This configuration is referred to as a "deep" architecture with k layers (see Figure 1 for an example).

For feature generation, we present a trained network with a new vector $\vec{x}$ representing the input data on its input layer. After performing one iteration of forward-propagation through the network, we can then view the activation values in the hidden layers as dense, so-called "distributed representations" (features) of the input data. These features can in turn be passed to an output classifier layer to produce some tagging task of interest. Recent work in deep learning show state-of-the-art results in part-of-speech parsing, chunking and named-entity tagging (Collobert, 2011), however performance in more complex NLP tasks like entity and event disambiguation and semantic role labelling are still trailing behind.

[2]E.g. a "one-hot" 50,000-dimensional vector of input words, with a '1' indicating the presence of the word at that index, and a '0' everywhere else.

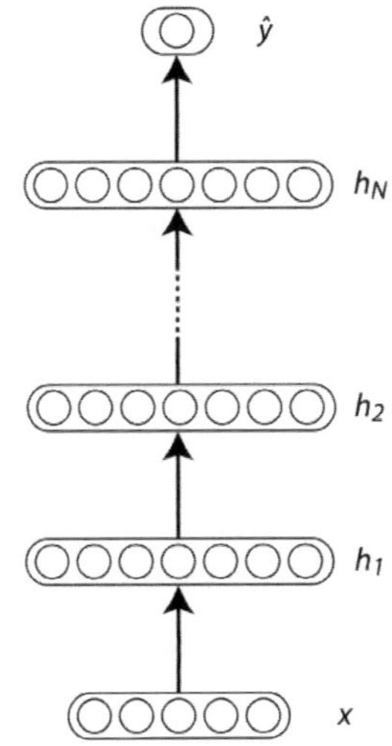

Figure 1: Example of a deep model. The input vector x is transformed into the hidden representation, here denoted as h_1, using an affine transformation W and a non-linearity. Each subsequent hidden layer h_k takes as input the output of its preceding layer $h_{(k-1)}$ (Bengio, 2009).

In this work we focus specifically on extending current state of the art deep neural models to improve their performance on these more difficult tasks. In the following section we briefly review and discuss the merits and limitations of three of the current state of the art deep learning models for NLP. We then identify our primary research questions and introduce our proposed future work roadmap.

2 Current State-of-the-Art and Limitations

Most work builds on the idea of a neural probabilistic language model (NPLM) where words are represented by learned real-valued embeddings, and a neural network combines word embeddings to predict the most likely next word. The first successful NPLM was introduced by Bengio et al. in 2003 (Bengio et al., 2003).

Historically, training and testing these models were slow, scaling linearly in the vocabulary size. However, several recent approaches have been proposed which overcome these limitations (Morin and Bengio, 2005), including the work by Collobert and Weston (2008) and Mnih and Hinton (2009) discussed next.

2.1 Collobert & Weston (2008)

Collobert and Weston (2008) present a discriminative, non-probabilistic, non-linear neural language model that can be scaled to train over billions of words since each training iteration only computes a loss gradient over a small stochastic sample of the training data.

All K-dimensional word embeddings are initially set to a random state. During each training iteration, an n-gram is read from the training data and each word is mapped to its respective embedding. All embeddings are then concatenated to form a nK-length positive training vector. A corrupted n-gram is also created by replacing the n'th (last) word by some word uniformly chosen from the vocabulary. The training criterion is that the network must predict positive training vectors with a score at least some margin higher than the score predicted for corrupted n-grams. Model parameters are trained *simultaneously* with word embeddings via gradient descent.

2.2 The Hierarchical Log Bilinear (HLBL) Model

Mnih and Hinton (2007) proposed a simple probabilistic linear neural language model called the log bilinear (LBL) model. For an n-gram context window, the LBL model concatenates the first $(n-1)$ K-dimensional word embeddings and then learns a linear mapping from $\mathbb{R}^{(n-1)K}$ to $\mathbb{R}^K$ for predicting the embedding of the nth word. For predicting the next word, the model outputs a probability distribution over the entire vocabulary by computing the dot product between the predicted embedding and the embedding for each word in the vocabulary in an output softmax layer. This softmax computation is linear in the length of the vocabulary for each prediction, and is therefore the performance bottleneck.

In follow-up work, Mnih and Hinton (2009) speed up training and testing time by extending the LBL model to predict the next word by hierarchically decomposing the search through the vocabulary by traversing a binary tree constructed over the vocabulary. This speeds up training and testing exponentially, but initially reduces model performance as the construction of the binary partitioning has a strong effect on the model's performance. They introduce a method for bootstrapping the construction of the tree by initially using a random binary tree to learn word embeddings, and then rebuilding the tree based on a clustering of the learned embeddings. Their final results are superior to the standard LBL in both model perplexity and model testing time.

2.3 Recursive Neural Networks (RNNs)

Socher (2010; 2011) introduces a recursive neural network (RNN) framework for parsing natural language. Previous approaches dealt with variable-length sentences by either

i using a window approach (shifting a window of n words over the input, processing each fixed-size window at a time), or

ii by using a convolutional layer where each word is convolved with its neighbours within some sentence- or window-boundary.

RNNs operate by recursively applying the same neural network to segments of its input, thereby allowing RNNs to naturally operate on variable-length inputs. Each pair of neighbouring words is scored by the network to reflect how likely these two words are considered to form part of a phrase. Each such operation takes two K-dimensional word vectors and outputs another K-dimensional vector and a score. Socher (2010) proposes several strategies (ranging from local and greedy to global and optimal) for choosing which pairs of words to collapse into a new K-dimensional vector representing the phrase comprised of the two words. By viewing these collapsing operations as branch merging decisions, one can construct a binary parse tree over the words in a bottom-up fashion.

2.4 Discussion of Limitations

Neural language models are appealing since they can more easily deal with missing data (unknown word combinations) due to their inherent continuous-space representation, whereas n-gram language models (Manning et al., 1999) need to employ (sometimes ad hoc) methods for *smoothing* unseen and hence zero probability word combinations.

The original NPLM performs well in terms of model perplexity on held-out data; however, its training and testing time is very slow. Furthermore, it provides no support for handling multiple word senses, the property that any word can have more than one meaning, since each word is assigned an embedding based on its literal string representation (i.e. from a lookup table).

The Collobert & Weston model still provides no mechanism for handling word senses, but improves on the NPLM by adding several non-linear layers which increase its modelling capacity, and a convolutional layer for modelling longer range dependencies between words. Recursive neural nets (RNNs) directly address the problem of longer-range dependencies by allowing neighbour words to be combined into their phrasal equivalents in a bottom-up process.

The LBL model, despite its very simple linear structure, provides very good performance in terms of model perplexity, but shares the problem of slow training and testing times and the inability to handle word senses or dependencies between words (outside its n-gram context).

In the HLBL model, Mnih and Hinton address the slow testing performance of the LBL model by using a hierarchical search tree over the vocabulary to exponentially speed up testing time, analogous to the concept of class-based language models (Brown et al., 1992). The HLBL model can also handle multiple word senses, but in their evaluation they show that in practice the model learns multiple senses (codes) for infrequently observed words instead of words with more than one meaning (Mnih and Hinton, 2009). The performance is strongly dependent on the initialisation of the tree, for which they present an iterative but non-optimal bootstrap-and-train procedure. Despite being non-optimal, it is shown to outperform the standard LBL model in terms of perplexity.

3 Mismatched Word Representations and Classifiers

The deep learning ideal is to train deep, non-linear models over large collections of unlabeled data, and then use these models to automatically extract information-rich, higher-level features[3] to integrate into standard NLP or image processing systems as added features to improve performance. However, several recent papers report surprising and seemingly contradicting results for this ideal.

In the most direct comparison for NLP, Turian (2010) compares features extracted using Brown clustering (a hierarchical clustering technique for clustering words based on their observed co-occurrence patterns), the hierarchical log-bilinear (HLBL) embeddings (Mnih and Hinton, 2007) and Collobert and Weston (C+W) embeddings (Collobert and Weston, 2008), by integrating these as additional features in standard supervised conditional random field (CRF) classification systems for NLP. Somewhat surprisingly, they find that using the more complex C+W and HLBL features do not improve significantly over Brown features. Indeed, under several conditions the Brown features give the best results.

These results are important for several reasons (we highlight these results in Table 2). The goal was to improve classification performance in structured prediction tasks in natural language by integrating features learned in a deep, unsupervised approach within a standard linear classification framework. Yet these complex, deep methods are outperformed by simpler unsupervised feature extraction methods.

[3]"Higher-level" features simply mean combining simpler features extracted from a text to produce conceptually more abstract indicators, e.g. combining word-indicators for "attack", "soldier", etc. to form an indicator for WAR, even though "war" is not mentioned anywhere in the text.

System	Dev	Test	MUC7
Baseline	90.03	84.39	67.48
HLBL 100-dim	92.00	88.13	75.25
C&W 50-dim	92.27	87.93	75.74
Brown, 1000 clusters	92.32	**88.52**	**78.84**
C&W 200-dim	**92.46**	87.96	75.51

Table 2: Final NER F1 results reported by Turian (2010).

In a sense, these seem to be negative results for the utility of deep learning in NLP. However, in this work we argue that these seemingly anomalous results stem from a mismatch between the feature learning function and the classifier that was used in the classification (and hence evaluation) process.

We consider the learning problem $h : \mathcal{X} \rightarrow \mathcal{Y}$ to decompose into $h = h'(\phi(\mathcal{X}))$, where ϕ is the feature learning function and h' is a standard supervised classifier. ϕ reads input from $\mathcal{X}$ and outputs encodings in feature space $\phi(x)$. h reads input in feature space $\phi(x)$ and outputs encodings in the output label space $\mathcal{Y}$.

Note that this easily extends to deep feature learning models by simply replacing $\phi(\mathcal{X})$ with $\phi^{(k)}(\cdots\phi^{(2)}(\phi^{(1)}(\mathcal{X}))\cdots)$, for a k-layer architecture, where the first layer reads input in $\mathcal{X}$ and each subsequent layer reads the output of the previous layer.

Within this view of the deep learning process, we can see that unsupervised feature learning does not happen in isolation. Instead, the learned features only make sense within some learning framework, since the output of the feature learning function ϕ (and each deep layer $\phi^{(k-1)}$) maps to a region in feature code space which becomes in turn the input to the output classifier h' (or subsequent layer $\phi^{(k)}$). We therefore argue that in a semi-supervised or unsupervised classification problem, the feature learning function ϕ should be strongly dependent on the classifier h' that interprets those features, and vice versa.

This notion ties in with the standard deep-learning training protocol of unsupervised pre-training followed by *joint* supervised fine-tuning (Hinton et al., 2006) of the top classification layer and the deeper feature extraction layers. We conjecture that jointly training a deep feature extraction model with a linear output classifier leads to better linearly separable feature vectors $\phi(x)$ than training both independently. Note that this is in contrast to how Turian (2010) integrated the unsupervised features into existing NLP systems via disjoint training.

4 Proposed Work and Research Questions

For simpler sequence tagging tasks such as part-of-speech tagging and noun phrase chunking, the state-of-the-art models introduced in Section 2 perform adequately. However, in order to make use of the increased modelling capacity of deep neural models, and to successfully model more complex semantic tasks such as anaphora resolution and semantic role labelling, *we hypothesise that the model needs to avoid modelling purely local lexical semantics and needs to efficiently handle multiple word senses and long-range dependencies between input words (or phrases) and output labels.* We propose to overcome the limitations of previous models with regard to these design goals, by focusing on the following key areas:

Input language representation: Neural models rely on vector representations of their input (as opposed to discrete representations as in, for instance, HMMs). In NLP, sentences are therefore encoded as real-valued embedding vectors. These vectors are learned in either a task-specific setting (as in the C+W model) or as part of a language model (as in the LBL model), where the goal is to predict the next word given the learned representations of the previous words. In order to maximise the information available to the model, we need to provide information-rich representations to the model. Current approaches represent each word in a sentence using a distinct word vector based on its literal string representation. However, as noted earlier, in NL the same words can have different senses based on the context in which it appears (polysemy). We propose to extend the hierarchical log-bilinear (HLBL) language model (see Section 2.2) in two important ways. We choose the HLBL model for its simplicity and good performance compared to more complex models.

Firstly, we propose to replace the iterative bootstrap-and-train process for learning the hierarchical tree structure over the vocabulary with a modified self-balancing binary tree. The tree rebalances itself from an initial random tree to leave most frequently accessed words near the root (for shorter codes and faster access times), while moving words between clusters to maximise overall model perplexity.

Secondly, we propose to add a word sense disambiguation layer capable of modelling long-range dependencies between input words. For this layer we will compare a modified RNN layer to a convolutional layer. The modified RNN will embed each focus word with its n most discriminative neighbour words (in a sentence context window) into a new K-dimensional, sense-disambiguated embedding vector for the focus word. We will evaluate and optimise the final model's learned representations by evaluating language model perplexity on held out data.

Model architecture and internal representation: Deep models derive their modelling power from their hierarchical structure. Each layer transforms the output representation of its previous layer, allowing the model to learn more general and abstract feature combinations in the higher layers which are relevant for the current task. The representations on the hidden layers serve as transformed feature representations of the input data for the output classifier. Enforcing sparsity on the hidden layers has been shown to produce stronger features for certain tasks in vision (Coates et al., 2010). Additionally, individual nodes might be highly correlated, which can also reduce the performance of certain classifiers which make strong independence assumptions (for instance naive Bayes). We propose to study the effect that enforcing sparsity in the learned feature representations has on task performance in NLP. Additionally, we propose to evaluate the effect that an even stronger training objective – one that encourages statistical independence between hidden nodes by learning factorial code representations (Hochreiter and Schmidhuber, 1999) – has on model performance.

Modelling structure in the output space: Tasks in NLP mostly involve predicting labels which exhibit highly regular structure. For instance, in part-of-speech tagging, two determiners have a very low likelihood of following directly on one another, e.g. "the the". In order to successfully model this phenomenon, a model must take into account previous (and potentially future) predictions when making the current prediction, e.g. as in hidden Markov models and conditional random fields. We propose to include sequential dependencies in the output labels and to compare this with including a convolutional layer below the output layer, for predicting output labels in complex NLP tasks such as coreference resolution and event structure detection.

5 Conclusion

Deep learning methods offer an attractive unsupervised approach for extracting higher-level features from large quantities of text data to be used for NLP tasks. However current attempts at integrating these features into existing NLP systems do not produce the desired performance improvements. We conjecture that this is due to a mismatch between the learned word representations and the classifiers used as a result of disjoint training schemes, and our thesis roadmap suggests three key areas for overcoming these limitations.

References

Y. Bengio, R. Ducharme, P. Vincent, and C. Janvin. 2003. A neural probabilistic language model. *Journal of Machine Learning Research*, 3:1137–1155, March.

Y. Bengio. 2009. Learning deep architectures for ai. *Foundations and Trends® in Machine Learning*, 2(1):1–127.

P.F. Brown, P.V. Desouza, R.L. Mercer, V.J.D. Pietra, and J.C. Lai. 1992. Class-based n-gram models of natural language. *Computational linguistics*, 18(4):467–479.

A. Coates, H. Lee, and A.Y. Ng. 2010. An analysis of single-layer networks in unsupervised feature learning. *Ann Arbor*, 1001:48109.

R. Collobert and J. Weston. 2008. A unified architecture for natural language processing: Deep neural networks with multitask learning. In *Proceedings of the 25th International Conference on Machine Learning*, pages 160–167. ACM.

R. Collobert. 2011. Deep learning for efficient discriminative parsing. In *International Conference on Artificial Intelligence and Statistics (AISTATS)*.

C. Cortes and V. Vapnik. 1995. Support-vector networks. *Machine learning*, 20(3):273–297.

D. Gildea and D. Jurafsky. 2002. Automatic labeling of semantic roles. *Computational Linguistics*, 28(3):245–288.

G.E. Hinton, S. Osindero, and Y.W. Teh. 2006. A fast learning algorithm for deep belief nets. *Neural computation*, 18(7):1527–1554.

S. Hochreiter and J. Schmidhuber. 1999. Feature extraction through lococode. *Neural Computation*, 11(3):679–714.

A. Hyvärinen, J. Karhunen, and E. Oja. 2001. *Independent component analysis*, volume 26. Wiley Interscience.

I.T. Jolliffe. 2002. *Principal component analysis*, volume 2. Wiley Online Library.

J. Lafferty. 2001. Conditional random fields: Probabilistic models for segmenting and labeling sequence data. In *Proceedings of ICML, 2001*.

S. Lloyd. 1982. Least squares quantization in pcm. *IEEE Transactions on Information Theory*, 28(2):129–137.

C.D. Manning, H. Schütze, and MITCogNet. 1999. *Foundations of statistical natural language processing*, volume 999. MIT Press.

A. Mnih and G. Hinton. 2007. Three new graphical models for statistical language modelling. In *Proceedings of the 24th international conference on Machine learning*, pages 641–648. ACM.

A. Mnih and G.E. Hinton. 2009. A scalable hierarchical distributed language model. *Advances in neural information processing systems*, 21:1081–1088.

F. Morin and Y. Bengio. 2005. Hierarchical probabilistic neural network language model. In *AISTATS05*, pages 246–252.

F. Rosenblatt. 1957. *The Perceptron, a Perceiving and Recognizing Automaton Project Para*. Cornell Aeronautical Laboratory.

C.E. Shannon and W. Weaver. 1962. *The mathematical theory of communication*, volume 19. University of Illinois Press Urbana.

R. Socher, C.D. Manning, and A.Y. Ng. 2010. Learning continuous phrase representations and syntactic parsing with recursive neural networks. In *Proceedings of the NIPS-2010 Deep Learning and Unsupervised Feature Learning Workshop*.

R. Socher, C.C. Lin, A.Y. Ng, and C.D. Manning. 2011. Parsing natural scenes and natural language with recursive neural networks. In *Proceedings of the 26th International Conference on Machine Learning (ICML)*, volume 2, page 7.

J. Turian, L. Ratinov, and Y. Bengio. 2010. Word representations: A simple and general method for semi-supervised learning. In *Proceedings of the 48th Annual Meeting of the Association for Computational Linguistics*, pages 384–394. Association for Computational Linguistics.

Automatic Metrics for Genre-specific Text Quality

Annie Louis
University of Pennsylvania
Philadelphia, PA 19103, USA
lannie@seas.upenn.edu

Abstract

To date, researchers have proposed different ways to compute the readability and coherence of a text using a variety of lexical, syntax, entity and discourse properties. But these metrics have not been defined with special relevance to any particular genre but rather proposed as general indicators of writing quality. In this thesis, we propose and evaluate novel text quality metrics that utilize the unique properties of different genres. We focus on three genres: academic publications, news articles about science, and machine generated text, in particular the output from automatic text summarization systems.

1 Introduction

Automatic methods to measure the writing quality of a text can be quite useful for several applications, for example search and recommendation systems, and writing support and grading tools. There are two main categories of prior work on this topic. The first is studies on 'readability' which have proposed metrics to select texts appropriate (easy to read) for an audience of given age and education level (Flesch, 1948; Collins-Thompson and Callan, 2004). These metrics typically classify texts as suitable for adult or child, or into a more fine-grained set of 12 educational grade levels. The second line of work are recent computational metrics to predict coherence. These methods identify regularities in words (Barzilay and Lee, 2004), entity coreference (Barzilay and Lapata, 2008) and discourse relations (Pitler and Nenkova, 2008) from a large collection of articles and use these patterns to predict the coherence. They assume a particular competency level (adult educated readers) and also fix the text (typically news articles, which are appropriate for adult readers). By removing the focus on age/education level, these methods compute textual differences between good and poorly written texts as perceived by a single audience level.

In my thesis, I propose a new definition – text quality: the overall well-written characteristic of an article. It differs from prior work in three respects:

1. We consider a single fixed audience level and the texts that audience is typically exposed to. For example, a college educated reader of a newspaper might find some articles better written than others, even though he understands and can read nearly all of them with ease.

2. It is a holistic property of texts. At a minimum, at least four factors influence quality: the content/topic that is discussed, sentence level-grammaticality, discourse coherence and writing style. Here writing style refers to extra properties introduced into the text by the author but do not necessarily interfere with coherence if not provided. For example, the use of metaphors, examples and humour can have connections with quality. Previous work on coherence metrics do not consider these aspects.

3. Such a property would also have genre-specific dimensions: an academic article should above all be clear and a thriller-story should be fast-paced and interesting. Further even if the same

Proceedings of the NAACL HLT 2012 Student Research Workshop, pages 54–59,
Montréal, Canada, June 3-8, 2012.

quality aspect is relevant for multiple genres, it has higher weight in one versus another. Prior readability and coherence studies were not proposed with relvance to any particular genre.

These aspects make the investigation of text quality linguistically interesting because by definition the focus is on a wide range of properties of the text itself rather than appropriateness for a reader.

In this thesis, we propose computable measures to capture genre-specific text quality. Our hypothesis is that writing quality is a combination some generic aspects that matter for most texts, such as grammatical sentences, and other unique ones which have high impact in a particular genre.

Specifically, we consider three genres which have high relevance for writing quality research—academic writing, science journalism and output of automatic summarization systems.

Both academic writing and science news articles describe science, but their audience is quite different. Academic writing aims to clearly explain the details of the research to other experts, while science news conveys interesting research findings to lay readers. This fact creates distinctive content and writing style in the two genres. There is also a huge opportunity in these genres for developing applications involving text quality, for example, authoring tools for academic writing and information retrival and recommendation for news articles. We also include a third genre—automatically generated summaries. Here, when systems produce multi-sentence text, they must ensure that the text is readable and coherent. Automatic evaluation of content and linguistic quality is therefore necessary for system development in this genre.

2 Thesis Summary and Contributions

For this thesis, we only consider the discourse and style components of text quality, aspects that have received less focus in prior work. Sentence-level problems have been widely explored and recently, even specifically for academic writing (Dale and Kilgarriff, 2010). We also do not consider content in our work, for example, academic writing quality also depends on the ideas and arguments presented but these aspects are outside the scope of this thesis. As defined previously, we focus on a fixed audience level. We assume a reader at the top level of the competency spectrum: an adult educated reader for science news and automatic summaries, and for academic articles, an expert on the topic. This definition has minimal focus on reader abilities and allows us to analyze textual differences exclusively.

The specific contributions of this thesis are:

1. Defining text quality in terms of linguistic aspects rather than readability: Our work is the first to propose a quality definition where well-written nature is the central focus and including genre-dependent aspects and writing style.

2. Investigating genre-specific metrics: This study is also the first to design and evaluate genre-specific features for text quality prediction. For each genre: academic writing, science journalism and automatic summaries, we develop metrics unique to the genre and evaluate their ability to predict text quality both individually and in combination with generic features put forth in prior work.

3. Proposing new discourse-level features: In prior work, there are discourse-based features based on coreference, discourse relations and word co-occurrence between adjacent sentences. We introduce new features which capture aspects such as organization of communicative goals and general-specific nature of sentences.

Specifically, we introduce the following metrics:

a) Patterns in communicative goals (Section 5): Every text has a purpose and the author uses a sequence of communicative goals realized as sentences to convey that purpose. We introduce a metric that predicts coherence based on the size and sequence of communicative goals for a genre. This aspect is most relevant for research writing: academic and science journalism because there is a clear goal and well-defined purpose for these articles.

b) General-specific nature of sentences (Section 6): Some sentences in a text convey only general content, others provide details and a well-written text would have a certain balance between the two. Particularly, while creating summaries, there is a length contraint, so it cannot include all specific content but some information must be made more general. We introduce a method to predict the specificity for a sentence and examine how specificity and sequence of general-specific sentences is related to the quality of automatic summaries.

c) Information cohesiveness (Section 7): This idea is also proposed for automatic summaries, they must have a focus and present a small set of ideas with easy to understand links between them. We show that cohesiveness properties (computed automatically) of the source text to be summarized can be linked to the expected content quality of summaries that can be generated for that text. This work will be extended to analyze the relationship of cohesiveness with ratings of focus for the summaries.

d) Aspects of style (Section 8): Here we investigate metrics beyond coherence and related to extra features included in the article. We consider the genre of science journalism and investigate whether surprise-invoking sentence construction, visual descriptions and emotional content of the articles are also correlated with perceived quality.

We will evaluate our approaches in two ways:

1. We investigate the extent to which genre-specific metrics are indicative of text quality and whether they complement generic features.

2. We also examine how unique these metrics are for a given genre, for example: are surprising articles always considered well-written even if they are not science-news? For this analysis, we will consider a set of randomly selected news texts (no genre division) with text quality ratings. On this set, we will test the performance of generic and each set of genre-specific metrics. We expect that on this data, the generic features would be best with little improvement from the genre-specific metrics.

So far, we have designed some of the metrics that we described above and have found them to be predictive of writing quality. We will carry out extensive evaluation of these measures in future work.

3 Related work

Early readability metrics used sentence length, number of syllables in words and number of 'easy' words to distinguish texts from different grade levels (Flesch, 1948; Gunning, 1952; Dale and Chall, 1948). Other measures are based on word familiarity (Collins-Thompson and Callan, 2004; Si and Callan, 2001), difficulty of concepts (Zhao and Kan, 2010) and features of sentence syntax (Schwarm and Ostendorf, 2005). There are also readability studies for audience distinctions other than grade levels. Feng et al. (2009) consider adult readers with intellectual disability and therefore introduce features such as the number of entities a person should keep in working memory for that text and how far entity links stretch. Heilman et al. (2007) show that grammatical features make a bigger impact while predicting readability for second language learners in contrast to native speakers.

Newer coherence measures do not focus on reader abilities. They are typically run on news articles and assume an adult audience. They show that word co-occurrence (Soricut and Marcu, 2006), subtopic structure (Barzilay and Lee, 2004), discourse relations (Pitler and Nenkova, 2008; Lin et al., 2011) and coreference patterns (Barzilay and Lapata, 2008) learn from large corpora can be used to predict coherence.

But prior metrics are not proposed as unique to any genre. Some metrics using word patterns (Si and Callan, 2001; Barzilay and Lee, 2004) are domain-dependent in that they require documents from the target domain for training. But they can be trained for any domain in this manner.

However recent work show that genre-specific indicators could be quite useful for applications. McIntyre and Lapata (2009) automatically generate short children's stories using patterns of event and entity co-occurrences. They find that people judge their stories as better when the text is optimized not only for coherence and but also its interesting nature. They use a supervised approach to predict the interest value for a story during the generation process. Burstein et al. (2010) find that for predicting the coherence of student essays, better accuracies can be obtained by augmenting generic coherence metrics with features related to student writing such as word variety and spelling errors.

In my own work on automatic evaluation of summaries (Pitler et al., 2010), I have observed the impact of genre. We consider a corpus of summaries written by people and those produced by automatic systems. Psycholinguistic metrics previously proposed for analyzing coherence of human texts work successfully on human summaries but are less accurate for system summaries. Similarly, metrics which predict the fluency of machine translations accurately, work barely above baseline for judging the grammaticality of sentences from human summaries. But they give high accuracies on machine summary sentences. So for machine and human generated text, clearly different features matter.

4 Corpora for text quality

For the automatic summarization genre, several years of evaluation workshops organized by NIST[1] have created large-scale datasets of automatic summaries rated manually by people for content and linguistic quality. We utilize this data for our experiments but such corpora do not exist for other genres.

For academic writing, we plan to use a collection of biology journal articles marked with the impact factor of the journal. The intuition is that the popular journals are more competitive and so the writing is on average better than less impactful venues. It is however not a direct measure of text quality. For some of our experiments done so far, we have taken an approach that is common with prior studies on coherence (Barzilay and Lee, 2004; Barzilay and Lapata, 2008; Lin et al., 2011). We take an original article and create a random permutation of its sentences, the latter we consider as an incoherent article and the original version as coherent.

For science news, we expect that Amazon Mechanical Turk will be a suitable platform for obtaining ratings of popular and interesting articles from the target audience. We also plan to use proxies such as lists of most emailed/viewed articles from news websites. Here the negative examples would be other articles published during the *same* day/period but not appearing in the popular article list.

5 Patterns in communicative goals

Consider the related work section of a conference paper. One might suppose that a good structure for this section would contain a description of an attribute of the current work, followed by previous work on the topic and then reporting how the current work is different and addresses shortcomings if any of prior work. In fact, this intuition of seeing texts as a sequence of semantic zones is well-understood for the academic writing genre. Prior research has identified that a small set of argumentative zones exist in academic articles such as motivation, results, prior work, speculations and descriptions. They also found that sentences could be manually annotated into zones with high agreement and automatically predicting the zone for a sentence can also be done with high accuracy (Teufel and Moens, 2000; Liakata et al., 2010). We hypothesize that these zones would also have a certain distribution and sequence in well-written articles versus others and propose a metric based on this aspect for the academic writing and science journalism genres.

Rather than using a predefined set of communicative goals, we develop an unsupervised technique to identify analogs to semantic zones and use the patterns in zones to predict coherence (Louis and Nenkova, 2012a). Our key idea is that the syntax of a sentence can be a useful proxy for its communicative goal. For example, questions and definition sentences have unique syntax. We extend this idea to a large scale analysis. Our model represents a sentence either using productions from its constituency parse tree or as a sequence of phrasal nodes. Then we employ two methods that learn patterns in these representations from a collection of articles. The first local method detects patterns in the syntax of adjacent sentences. The second approach is global, where sentences are first grouped into clusters based on syntactic similarity and a Hidden Markov Model is used to record patterns. Each hidden state is assumed to generate the syntax of sentences from a particular zone.

We have evaluated our method on conference publications from the ACL anthology. Our results indicate that we can distinguish an original introduction, abstract or related work section from a corresponding perturbed version (where the sentences are randomly permuted and is therefore incoherent text) with accuracies of 64 to 74% over a 50% baseline.

6 General-specific nature of sentences

In any article, some sentences convey the topic at a high level with other sentences providing details such as justification and examples. The idea is particularly relevant for summaries. Since summaries are much shorter than their source documents, they cannot include all the details from the source. Some details have to be omitted and others made more general. So we explore the preferred degree of general-specific content and its relationship to text quality for summaries.

[1] http://www.nist.gov/tac/

We developed a classifier to distinguish between general and specific sentences from news articles (Louis and Nenkova, 2011a; Louis and Nenkova, 2012b). The classifier uses features such as the word specificity, presence of named entities, word polarity, counts of different phrase types, sentence length, likelihood under language models and the identities of the words themselves. For example, sentences with named entities tended to be specific whereas sentences with shorter verb phrases and more polarity words were general. This classifier was trained on sentences multiply annotated by people as general or specific and produces an accuracy of about 79%. Further the classifier confidence was found to be indicative of the annotator agreement on the sentences; when there was high agreement that a sentence was either general or specific, the classifier also made a very confident prediction for the correct class. So our system also provides a graded score for specificity rather than binary predictions.

Using the classifier we analyzed a large corpus of news summaries created by people and by automatic systems (Louis and Nenkova, 2011b). We found that summaries written by people have more general content than automatic summaries. Similarly, when people were asked to rate automatic summaries for content quality, they gave higher scores to general summaries than specific. On the linguistic quality side an opposite trend was found. Summaries that were more specific had higher scores. Our examinations revealed that general sentences, since they are topic oriented and high level, need to be followed by proper substantiation and details. But automatic systems are rather poor at achieving such ordering. So even though more general content is preferred in summaries, proper ordering of general-specific sentences is needed to create the right effect.

7 Information cohesiveness

If an article has too many ideas it would be difficult to read. Also if the ideas were not closely related in the article that would create additional difficulty. This aspect is important for machine generated text: an automatic summary should focus on a few main aspects rather than present a bag of many unrelated facts. In fact, in large scale evaluation workshops, automatic summaries are also manually graded for a 'focus' aspect. For this purpose, we want to identify metrics which can indicate cohesiveness and focus of an article. In our studies so far, we have have developed cohesiveness metrics for clusters of articles (Nenkova and Louis, 2008; Louis and Nenkova, 2009). In future work, we will explore how these metrics work for individual articles.

Information quality also arises in the context of source documents given for automatic summarization. Particularly for systems which summarize online news, the input is created by clustering together news on the same topic from different sources. For example, a cluster may be created for the Japanese earthquake and aftermath. When the period covered is too large or when the documents discuss many different opinions and ideas it becomes hard for a system to point out the most relevant facts. So one proxy for cohesiveness of the input cluster is the average quality of a number of automatic summaries produced for it by different methods. If most of these methods fail to produce a good summary, then that input can be deemed as difficult and incohesive.

We used a large collection of inputs, their automatic summaries and summary scores from the DUC workshops. We computed the average content quality score given by people to each summary and computed the average performance on summaries created for the same input. This value represents the expected system performance for that input and we develop features to predict the same. We simplify the task as binary prediction, average system performance above mean value – low difficulty, and high difficulty otherwise.

One indicative feature was the entropy of the distribution of words in the input. When the entropy was low, the difficulty was less since there are few main ideas to summarize. Another useful feature was the divergence computed between the word distribution in an input and that of a random collection of documents not on any topic. If the input distribution was closer to random documents it indicates the lack of a coherent topic for the source cluster and such inputs were under the hard category. We envision that similar features might help to predict judgements of focus for automatic summaries.

8 Current and future work

For future work, we want to focus on metrics related to style of writing. We will do this analysis for science news articles since journalists employ creative ways to convey technical research content to non-experts readers. For example, authors use analogies and visual language and incorporate a story line. We also noticed that some of the most emailed articles are entertaining and even contain humor. Two example snippets from such articles are provided below to demonstrate some of our intuitions about text quality in this genre. Our aim is to obtain lexical and syntactic correlates that capture some of these unique factors for this domain.

[1]... caused by defects in the cilia—solitary slivers that poke out of almost every cell in the body. They are not the wisps that wave Rockette-like in our airways.

[2] News flash: we're boring. New research that makes creative use of sensitive location-tracking data from cellphones in Europe suggests that most people can be found in one of just a few locations at any time.

Future work will also include extensive evaluation of our proposed models.

References

R. Barzilay and M. Lapata. 2008. Modeling local coherence: An entity-based approach. *Computational Linguistics*, 34(1):1–34.

R. Barzilay and L. Lee. 2004. Catching the drift: Probabilistic content models, with applications to generation and summarization. In *Proceedings of NAACL-HLT*, pages 113–120.

J. Burstein, J. Tetreault, and S. Andreyev. 2010. Using entity-based features to model coherence in student essays. In *Proceedings of HLT-NAACL*, pages 681–684.

K. Collins-Thompson and J. Callan. 2004. A language modeling approach to predicting reading difficulty. In *Proceedings of HLT-NAACL*, pages 193–200.

E. Dale and J. S. Chall. 1948. A formula for predicting readability. *Edu. Research Bulletin*, 27(1):11–28.

R. Dale and A. Kilgarriff. 2010. Helping our own: text massaging for computational linguistics as a new shared task. In *Proceedings of INLG*, pages 263–267.

L. Feng, N. Elhadad, and M. Huenerfauth. 2009. Cognitively motivated features for readability assessment. In *Proceedings of EACL*, pages 229–237.

R. Flesch. 1948. A new readability yardstick. *Journal of Applied Psychology*, 32:221 – 233.

R. Gunning. 1952. *The technique of clear writing*. McGraw-Hill; Fouth Printing edition.

M. Heilman, K. Collins-Thompson, J. Callan, and M. Eskenazi. 2007. Combining lexical and grammatical features to improve readability measures for first and second language texts. In *Proceedings of HLT-NAACL*, pages 460–467.

M. Liakata, S. Teufel, A. Siddharthan, and C. Batchelor. 2010. Corpora for the conceptualisation and zoning of scientific papers. In *Proceedings of LREC*.

Z. Lin, H. Ng, and M. Kan. 2011. Automatically evaluating text coherence using discourse relations. In *Proceedings of ACL-HLT*, pages 997–1006.

A. Louis and A. Nenkova. 2009. Performance confidence estimation for automatic summarization. In *Proceedings of EACL*, pages 541–548.

A. Louis and A. Nenkova. 2011a. Automatic identification of general and specific sentences by leveraging discourse annotations. In *Proceedings of IJCNLP*, pages 605–613.

A. Louis and A. Nenkova. 2011b. Text specificity and impact on quality of news summaries. In *Proceedings of the Workshop on Monolingual Text-To-Text Generation*, pages 34–42.

A. Louis and A. Nenkova. 2012a. A coherence model based on syntactic patterns. *Technical Report, University of Pennsylvania*.

A. Louis and A. Nenkova. 2012b. A corpus of general and specific sentences from news. In *Proceedings of LREC*.

N. McIntyre and M. Lapata. 2009. Learning to tell tales: A data-driven approach to story generation. In *Proceedings of ACL-IJCNLP*, pages 217–225.

A. Nenkova and A. Louis. 2008. Can you summarize this? identifying correlates of input difficulty for multi-document summarization. In *Proceedings of ACL-HLT*, pages 825–833.

E. Pitler and A. Nenkova. 2008. Revisiting readability: A unified framework for predicting text quality. In *Proceedings of EMNLP*, pages 186–195.

E. Pitler, A. Louis, and A. Nenkova. 2010. Automatic evaluation of linguistic quality in multi-document summarization. In *Proceedings of ACL*.

S. Schwarm and M. Ostendorf. 2005. Reading level assessment using support vector machines and statistical language models. In *Proceedings of ACL*, pages 523–530.

L. Si and J. Callan. 2001. A statistical model for scientific readability. In *Proceedings of CIKM*, pages 574–576.

R. Soricut and D. Marcu. 2006. Discourse generation using utility-trained coherence models. In *Proceedings of COLING-ACL*, pages 803–810.

S. Teufel and M. Moens. 2000. What's yours and what's mine: determining intellectual attribution in scientific text. In *Proceedings of EMNLP*, pages 9–17.

J. Zhao and M. Kan. 2010. Domain-specific iterative readability computation. In *Proceedings of JDCL*, pages 205–214.

A Weighting Scheme for Open Information Extraction

Yuval Merhav
Illinois Institute of Technology
Chicago, IL USA
`yuval@ir.iit.edu`

Abstract

We study[1] the problem of extracting all possible relations among named entities from unstructured text, a task known as Open Information Extraction (Open IE). A state-of-the-art Open IE system consists of natural language processing tools to identify entities and extract sentences that relate such entities, followed by using text clustering to identify the relations among co-occurring entity pairs. In particular, we study how the current weighting scheme used for Open IE affects the clustering results and propose a term weighting scheme that significantly improves on the state-of-the-art in the task of relation extraction both when used in conjunction with the standard $tf \cdot idf$ scheme, and also when used as a pruning filter.

1 Introduction

The extraction of structured information from text is a long-standing challenge in Natural Language Processing which has been re-invigorated with the ever-increasing availability of user-generated textual content online. The large-scale extraction of unknown relations has been termed as Open Information Extraction (Open IE) (Banko et al., 2007) (also referred to as Open Relationship Extraction, Relation Extraction, or Relation Discovery). Many challenges exist in developing an Open IE solution, such as recognizing and disambiguating entities in a multi-document setting, and identifying all so-called *relational* terms in the sentences connecting pairs of entities. Relational terms are words (usually one or two) that describe a relation between entities (for instance, terms like "running mate", "opponent", "governor of" are relational terms).

[1]This thesis proposal has been accepted for publication in (Merhav et al., 2012).

One approach for Open IE is based on clustering of entity pairs to produce relations, as introduced by Hasegawa et al. (Hasegawa et al., 2004). Their and follow-up works (e.g., (Mesquita et al., 2010)) extract terms in a small window between two named entities to build the context vector of each entity pair, and then apply a clustering algorithm to cluster together entity pairs that share the same relation (e.g., `Google–Youtube` and `Google–Motorola Mobility` in a cluster about the "acquired" relation). Contexts of entity pairs are represented using the vector space model. The state-of-the-art in clustering-based Open IE assigns weights to the terms according to the standard $tf{\cdot}idf$ scheme.

Motivation. Intuitively, the justification for using idf is that a term appearing in many documents (i.e., many contexts in our setting) would not be a good *discriminator* (Robertson, 2004), and thus should weigh proportionally less than other, more *rare* terms. For the task of relation extraction however, we are interested specifically in terms that describe relations. In our settings, a single document is a context vector of one entity pair, generated from all articles discussing this pair, which means that the fewer entity pairs a term appears in, the higher its idf score would be. Consequently, it is not necessarily the case that terms that are associated with high idf weights would be good relation discriminators. On the other hand, popular relational terms that ap-

Proceedings of the NAACL HLT 2012 Student Research Workshop, pages 60–65,
Montréal, Canada, June 3-8, 2012.

ply to many entity pairs would have relatively lower *idf* weights.

It is natural to expect that the relations extracted by an Open IE system are strongly correlated with a given context. For instance, marriage is a relation between two persons and thus belongs to the domain PER–PER. We exploit this observation to boost the weight of relational terms associated with marriage (e.g., "wife", "spouse", etc.) in those entity pairs where the domain is also PER–PER. The more dominant a term in a given domain compared to other domains, the higher its boosting score would be.

Our work resembles the work on selectional preferences (Resnik, 1996). Selectional preferences are semantic constraints on arguments (e.g. a verb like "eat" prefers as object edible things).

2 Related Work

Different approaches for Open IE have been proposed in the literature, such as bootstrapping (e.g., (Zhu et al., 2009) (Bunescu and Mooney, 2007)), self or distant supervision (e.g., (Banko et al., 2007) (Mintz et al., 2009)) and rule based (e.g., (Fader et al., 2011)). In this work we focus on unsupervised approaches.

Fully unsupervised Open IE systems are mainly based on clustering of entity pair contexts to produce clusters of entity pairs that share the same relations, as introduced by Hasegawa et al. (Hasegawa et al., 2004) (this is the system we use in this work as our baseline). Hasegawa et al. used word unigrams weighted by $tf \cdot idf$ to build the context vectors and applied Hierarchical Agglomerative Clustering (HAC) with complete linkage deployed on a 1995 New York Times corpus. Mesquita et al. extended this work by using other features such as part of speech patterns (Mesquita et al., 2010). To reduce noise in the feature space, a common problem with text mining, known feature selection and ranking methods for clustering have been applied (Chen et al., 2005; Rosenfeld and Feldman, 2007). Both works used the K-Means clustering algorithm with the stability-based criterion to automatically estimate the number of clusters.

This work extends all previous clustering works by utilizing domain frequency as a novel weighting scheme for clustering entity pairs. The idea of domain frequency was first proposed for predicting entities which are erroneously typed by NER systems (Merhav et al., 2010).

3 Data and Evaluation

This work was implemented on top of the SONEX system (Mesquita et al., 2010), deployed on the ICWSM 2009 Spinn3r corpus (Burton et al., 2009), focusing on posts in English (25 million out of 44 million in total), collected between August 1st, 2008 and October 1st, 2008. The system uses the Illinois Entity Tagger (Ratinov and Roth, 2009) and Orthomatcher from the GATE framework[2] for within-a-document co-reference resolution.

Evaluating Open IE systems is a difficult problem. Mesquita et al. evaluated SONEX by automatically matching a sample of the entity pairs their system identified from the Spinn3r corpus against a publicly available curated database[3]. Their approach generated two datasets: INTER and 10PERC. INTER contains the intersection pairs only (i.e., intersection pairs are those from Spinn3r and Freebase that match both entity names and types exactly), while 10PERC contains 10% of the total pairs SONEX identified, including the intersection pairs. We extended these two datasets by adding more entity pairs and relations. We call the resulting datasets INTER (395 entity pairs and 20 different relations) and NOISY (contains INTER plus approximately 30,000 entity pairs as compared to the 13,000 pairs in 10PERC).

We evaluate our system by reporting f-measure numbers for our system running on INTER and NOISY against the ground truth, using similar settings used by (Hasegawa et al., 2004) and (Mesquita et al., 2010). These include word unigrams as features, HAC with average link (outperformed single and complete link), and $tf \cdot idf$ and cosine similarity as the baseline.

4 Weighting Scheme

Identifying the relationship (if any) between entities e_1, e_2 is done by analyzing the sentences that mention e_1 and e_2 together. An *entity pair* is defined by two entities e_1 and e_2 together with the *context* in

[2]http://gate.ac.uk/

[3]http://www.freebase.com

which they co-occur. For our purposes, the context can be any textual feature that allows the identification of the relationship for the given pair. The contexts of entity pairs are represented using the vector space model with the common $tf \cdot idf$ weighting scheme. More precisely, for each term t in the context of an entity pair, tf is the frequency of the term in the context, while

$$idf = \log\left(\frac{|D|}{|d : t \in d|}\right),$$

where $|D|$ is the total number of entity pairs, and $|d : t \in d|$ is the number of entity pairs containing term t. The standard cosine similarity is used to compute the similarity between context vectors during clustering.

4.1 Domain Frequency

We start with a motivating example before diving into the details about how we compute *domain frequency*. We initially built our system with the traditional $tf \cdot idf$ and were unsatisfied with the results. Consequently, we examined the data to find a better way to score terms and filter noise. For example, we noticed that the pair *Youtube[ORG] – Google[ORG]* (associated with the "Acquired by" relation) was not clustered correctly. In Table 1 we listed all the Unigram features we extracted for the pair from the entire collection sorted by their domain frequency score for `ORG–ORG` (recall that these are the intervening features between the pair for each co-occurrence in the entire dataset). For clarity the terms were not stemmed.

Clearly, most terms are irrelevant which make it difficult to cluster the pair correctly. We listed in bold all terms that we think are useful. Besides "belongs", all these terms have high domain frequency scores. However, most of these terms do not have high idf scores. Term frequencies within a pair are also not helpful in many cases since many pairs are mentioned only a few times in the text. Next, we define the domain frequency score (Merhav et al., 2010).

Definition. Let P be the set of entity pairs, let T be the set of all entity types, and let $D = T \times T$ be the set of all possible relation domains. The *domain frequency* (df) of a term t, appearing in the context of some entity pair in P, in a given relation domain $i \in D$, denoted $df_i(t)$, is defined as

$$df_i(t) = \frac{f_i(t)}{\sum_{1 \leq j \leq n} f_j(t)},$$

where $f_i(t)$ is the frequency with which term t appears in the context of entity pairs of domain $i \in D$, and n is the number of domains in D. When computing the df score for a given term, it is preferred to consider each pair only once. For example, *"Google[ORG] acquired Youtube[ORG]"* would be counted only once (for "acquired" in the `ORG–ORG` domain) even if this pair and context appear many times in the collection. By doing so we eliminate the problem of duplicates (common on the web).

Unlike the idf score, which is a *global* measure of the discriminating power of a term, the df score is domain-specific. Thus, intuitively, the df score would favour specific relational terms (e.g., "wife" which is specific to personal relations) as opposed to generic ones (e.g., "member of" which applies to several domains). To validate this hypothesis, we computed the df scores of several relational terms found in the clusters the system produced on the main Spinn3r corpus.

Figure 1 shows the relative df scores of 4 relational terms (**mayor**, **wife**, **CEO**, and **coach**) which illustrate well the strengths of the df score. We can see that for the majority of terms (Figure 1(a)–(c)), there is a single domain for which the term has a clearly dominant df score: `LOC–PER` for **mayor**, `PER–PER` for **wife**, and `ORG–PER` for **CEO**.

Dependency on NER Types. Looking again at Figure 1, there is one case in which the df score does not seem to discriminate a reasonable domain. For **coach**, the dominant domain is `LOC–PER`, which can be explained by the common use of the city (or state) name as a proxy for a team as in the sentence "Syracuse football coach Greg Robinson". Note, however, that the problem in this case is the difficulty for the NER to determine that "Syracuse" refers to the university. These are some examples of correctly identified pairs in the **coach** relation but in which the NER types are misleading:

- `LOC–PER` domain: (England, Fabio Capello); (Croatia, Slaven Bilic); (Sunderland, Roy Keane).

Table 1: Unigram features for the pair *Youtube[ORG] – Google[ORG]* with *idf* and *df* (ORG–ORG) scores

Term	*idf*	*df* **(ORG–ORG)**	**Term**	*idf*	*df* **(ORG–ORG)**
ubiquitious	11.6	1.00	blogs	6.4	0.14
sale	5.9	0.80	services	5.9	0.13
parent	6.8	0.78	instead	4.0	0.12
uploader	10.5	0.66	free	5.0	0.12
purchase	6.3	0.62	similar	5.7	0.12
add	6.1	0.33	recently	4.2	0.12
traffic	7.0	0.55	disappointing	8.2	0.12
downloader	10.9	0.50	dominate	6.4	0.11
dailymotion	9.5	0.50	hosted	5.6	0.10
bought	5.2	0.49	hmmm	9.3	0.10
buying	5.8	0.47	giant	5.4	< 0.1
integrated	7.3	0.44	various	5.7	< 0.1
partnership	6.7	0.42	revealed	5.2	< 0.1
pipped	8.9	0.37	experiencing	7.7	< 0.1
embedded	7.6	0.36	fifth	6.5	< 0.1
add	6.1	0.33	implication	8.5	< 0.1
acquired	5.6	0.33	owner	6.0	< 0.1
channel	6.3	0.28	corporate	6.4	< 0.1
web	5.8	0.26	comments	5.2	< 0.1
video	4.9	0.24	according	4.5	< 0.1
sellout	9,2	0.23	resources	6.9	< 0.1
revenues	8.6	0.21	grounds	7.8	< 0.1
account	6.0	0.18	poked	6.9	< 0.1
evading	9.8	0.16	**belongs**	6.2	< 0.1
eclipsed	7.8	0.16	authors	7.4	< 0.1
company	4.7	0.15	hooked	7.1	< 0.1

- `MISC–PER` domain: (Titans, Jeff Fisher); (Jets, Eric Mangini); (Texans, Gary Kubiak).

4.2 Using the *df* Score

We use the *df* score for two purposes in our work. First, for clustering, we compute the weights of the terms inside all vectors using the product $tf{\cdot}idf \cdot df$. Second, we also use the *df* score as a filtering tool, by removing terms from vectors whenever their *df* scores lower than a threshold. Going back to the *Youtube[ORG] – Google[ORG]* example in Table 1, we can see that minimum *df* filtering helps with removing many noisy terms. We also use maximum *idf* filtering which helps with removing terms that have high *df* scores only because they are rare and appear only within one domain (e.g., ubiquitious (misspelled in source) and uploader in this example).

As we shall see in the experimental evaluation, even in the presence of incorrect type assignments made by the NER tool, the use of *df* scores improves the accuracy significantly. It is also worth mentioning that computing the *df* scores can be done fairly efficiently, and as soon as all entity pairs are extracted.

5 Results

We now report the results on INTER and NOISY. Our baseline run is similar to the systems published by Hasegawa et al. (Hasegawa et al., 2004) and Mesquita et al. (Mesquita et al., 2010); that is HAC with average link using $tf \cdot idf$ and cosine similarity, and stemmed word unigrams (excluding stop words) as features extracted using a window size of five words between pair of entities. Figure 2 shows that by integrating domain frequency

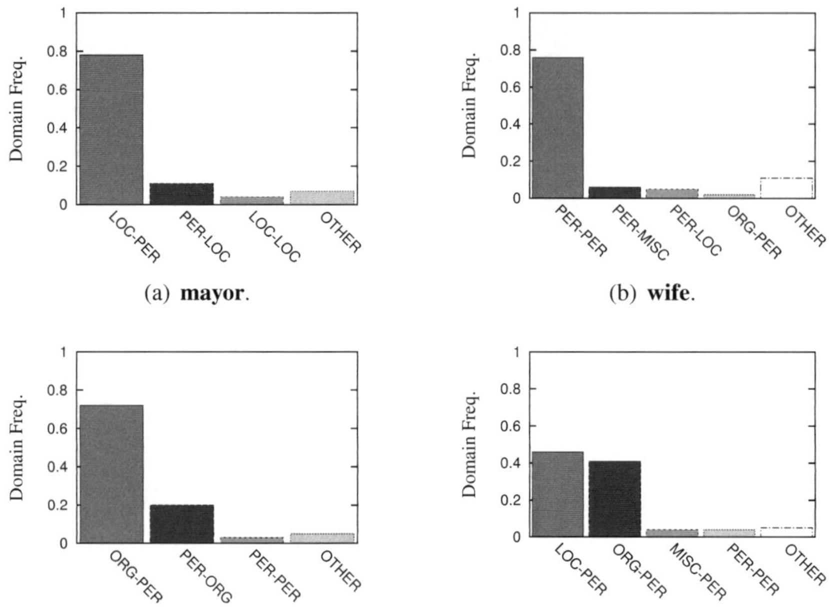

(a) **mayor**. (b) **wife**.

(c) **CEO**. (d) **coach**.

Figure 1: Domain Frequency examples.

(df) we significantly outperformed this baseline on both datasets (INTER: F-1 score of 0.87 compared to 0.75; NOISY: F-1 score of 0.72 compared to 0.65). In addition, filtering terms by minimum *df* and maximum *idf* thresholds improved the results further on INTER. These results are promising since a major challenge in text clustering is reducing the noise in the data.

We also see a substantial decrease of the results on NOISY compared to INTER. Such a decrease is, of course, expected: NOISY contains not only thousands more entity pairs than INTER, but also hundreds (if not thousands) more *relations* as well, making the clustering task harder in practice.

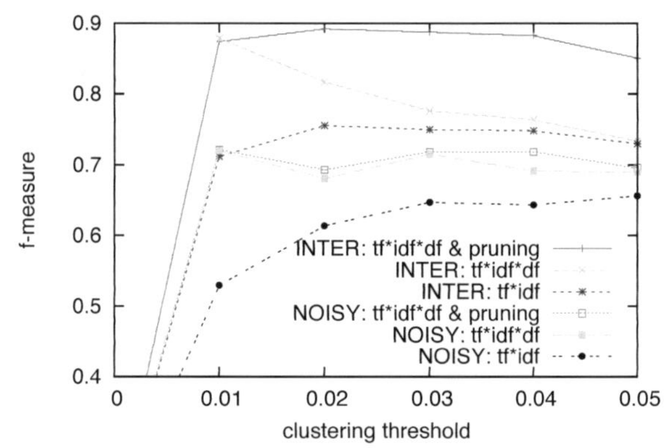

Figure 2: $tf \times idf$ Vs. $tf \times idf \times df$ with and without minimum *df* and maximum *idf* pruning on INTER and NOISY. All results consistently dropped for clustering thresholds larger than 0.05.

6 Conclusion and Future Research Directions

We utilized the Domain Frequency (*df*) score as a term-weighting score designed for identifying relational terms for Open IE. We believe that *df* can be utilized in various of applications, with the advantage that in practice, for many such applications, the list of terms and scores can be used off-the-shelf with no further effort. One such application is Named Entity Recognition (NER) – *df* helps in identifying relational patterns that are associated with a certain domain (e.g., PER–PER). If the list of words and phrases associated with their *df* scores is generated using an external dataset annotated with entities, it can be applied to improve results in other, more difficult domains, where the performance of the NER is poor.

It is also appealing that the *df* score is probabilistic, and as such, it is, for the most part, language independent. Obviously, not all languages have the same structure as English and some adjustments should be made. For example, *df* exploits the fact that relational verbs are usually placed between two entities in a sentence, which may not be always the case in other languages (e.g., German). Investigating how *df* can be extended and utilized in a multi-lingual environment is an interesting future direction.

7 Acknowledgements

The author would like to thank Professor Denilson Barbosa from the University of Alberta, Professor David Grossman and Gady Agam from Illinois Institute of Technology, and Professor Ophir Frieder from Georgetown University. All provided great help in forming the ideas that led to this work.

References

Michele Banko, Michael J. Cafarella, Stephen Soderland, Matthew Broadhead, and Oren Etzioni. 2007. Open information extraction from the web. In Manuela M. Veloso, editor, *IJCAI*, pages 2670–2676.

Razvan C. Bunescu and Raymond J. Mooney. 2007. Learning to extract relations from the web using minimal supervision. In *ACL*.

K. Burton, A. Java, and I. Soboroff. 2009. The icwsm 2009 spinn3r dataset. In *Proceedings of the Annual Conference on Weblogs and Social Media*.

Jinxiu Chen, Donghong Ji, Chew Lim Tan, and Zhengyu Niu. 2005. Unsupervised feature selection for relation extraction. In *IJCNLP-05: The 2nd International Joint Conference on Natural Language Processing*. Springer.

Anthony Fader, Michael Schmitz, Robert Bart, Stephen Soderland, and Oren Etzioni. 2011. Identifying relations for open information extraction. Manuscript submitted for publication. University of Washington.

Takaaki Hasegawa, Satoshi Sekine, and Ralph Grishman. 2004. Discovering relations among named entities from large corpora. In *ACL '04: Proceedings of the 42nd Annual Meeting on Association for Computational Linguistics*, page 415, Morristown, NJ, USA. Association for Computational Linguistics.

Yuval Merhav, Filipe Mesquita, Denilson Barbosa, Wai Gen Yee, and Ophir Frieder. 2010. Incorporating global information into named entity recognition systems using relational context. In *Proceedings of the 33rd international ACM SIGIR conference on Research and development in information retrieval*, SIGIR '10, pages 883–884, New York, NY, USA. ACM.

Yuval Merhav, Filipe Mesquita, Denilson Barbosa, Wai Gen Yee, and Ophir Frieder. 2012. Extracting information networks from the blogosphere. *ACM Transactions on the Web (TWEB)*. Accepted 2012.

Filipe Mesquita, Yuval Merhav, and Denilson Barbosa. 2010. Extracting information networks from the blogosphere: State-of-the-art and challenges. In *4th Int'l AAAI Conference on Weblogs and Social Media–Data Challenge*.

Mike Mintz, Steven Bills, Rion Snow, and Daniel Jurafsky. 2009. Distant supervision for relation extraction without labeled data. In *ACL-IJCNLP '09: Proceedings of the Joint Conference of the 47th Annual Meeting of the ACL and the 4th International Joint Conference on Natural Language Processing of the AFNLP: Volume 2*, pages 1003–1011, Morristown, NJ, USA. Association for Computational Linguistics.

Lev Ratinov and Dan Roth. 2009. Design challenges and misconceptions in named entity recognition. In *CoNLL '09: Proceedings of the Thirteenth Conference on Computational Natural Language Learning*, pages 147–155, Morristown, NJ, USA. Association for Computational Linguistics.

Philip Resnik. 1996. Selectional constraints: an information-theoretic model and its computational realization.

Stephen Robertson. 2004. Understanding inverse document frequency: On theoretical arguments for idf. *Journal of Documentation*, 60:2004.

Benjamin Rosenfeld and Ronen Feldman. 2007. Clustering for unsupervised relation identification. In *CIKM '07*, pages 411–418, New York, NY, USA. ACM.

Jun Zhu, Zaiqing Nie, Xiaojiang Liu, Bo Zhang, and Ji-Rong Wen. 2009. Statsnowball: a statistical approach to extracting entity relationships. In *Proceedings of the 18th international conference on World wide web*, WWW '09, pages 101–110, New York, NY, USA. ACM.

Automatic Humor Classification on Twitter

Yishay Raz
Shanghai Jiao Tong University
Department of Computer Science & Engineering
800 Dongchuan Road
Shanghai, 200024, China
yishayraz@yahoo.com

Abstract

Much has been written about humor and even sarcasm automatic recognition on Twitter. The task of classifying humorous tweets according to the type of humor has not been confronted so far, as far as we know. This research is aimed at applying classification and other NLP algorithms to the challenging task of automatically identifying the type and topic of humorous messages on Twitter. To achieve this goal, we will extend the related work surveyed hereinafter, adding different types of humor and characteristics to distinguish between them, including stylistic, syntactic, semantic and pragmatic ones. We will keep in mind the complex nature of the task at hand, which emanates from the informal language applied in tweets and variety of humor types and styles. These tend to be remarkably different from the type specific ones recognized in related works. We will use semi-supervised classifiers on a dataset of humorous tweets driven from different Twitter humor groups or funny tweet sites. Using a Mechanical Turk we will create a gold standard in which each tweet will be tagged by several annotators, in order to achieve an agreement between them, although the nature of the humor might allow one tweet to be classified under more than one class and topic of humor.

1 Introduction

The interaction between humans and machines has long extended out of the usability aspect. Nowadays, computers are not merely a tool to extend our lacking memory and manpower, but also serve a larger role in communications, entertainment and motivation. These may be found in such systems as Chatterbots, gaming and decision making. Humor is extremely important in any communicative form. It affects not only feelings but also influences human beliefs. It has even shown to encourage creativity. Enabling a machine to classify humor types (and topics) can have many practical applications, such as automatic humor subscriptions that send us only those messages that will make us laugh. It can serve as a basis for further research on humor generation of witty and adequate replies by conversational agent applications. We tend to expose more about ourselves in humor than in regular prose. In the next section we will highlight several research results from the fields of psychology and sociology that show this, and explore the differences in humor produced by different groups. This knowledge can be used to identify the latent attributes of the tweeters, e.g. gender, geographical location or origin and personality features based on their tweets. Aggressiveness in humor can be viewed as a potential warning sign and teach us about the authors mental well-being.

We will now look at some examples of funny tweets from one of the sites, and then review the different types, topics and the way in which the human brain operates to get the joke. We will also see how computers can imitate this:

1. "And he said unto his brethren, A man shall not poketh another man on facebook for thine is gayeth" #lostbibleverses

2. if life gives you lemons, make someone's paper

Proceedings of the NAACL HLT 2012 Student Research Workshop, pages 66–70,
Montréal, Canada, June 3-8, 2012. ©2012 Association for Computational Linguistics

cut really sting

3. Sitting at a coffee bean and watching someone get arrested at the starbucks across the street. True story.

4. One of Tigers mistresses got 10 million dollars to keep quiet. I gotta admit I'm really proud of that whore.

5. There is a new IPod app that translates Jay Leno into funny.

6. May the 4th be with you...

Example (1) has a hashtag that could help us understand the special stylistic suffixes some words in the sentence bear. Googling the first part yields more than 2 million hits, since this is a common biblical verse. This makes it a wordplay joke that paraphrases a known phrase. But the main reason this is funny is the observation that a very common Facebook action is gay. Therefore, the type of this humor would be classified as observational and the topic Facebook. The latter could be observed by a computer if we allow it to recognize the named entity facebook, which in many cases would serve as the topic. The type, which we recognize as gay, will appear in our lexicon. Since it appears after a copula, we can infer that this is not a regular gay joke. If it was an outing tweet it would not be funny. For both processes, we require a part of speech tagger and a NE recognizer. We can find these two tools at tt http://www.cs.washington.edu/homes/aritter/, developed especially for Twitter by Alan Ritter. Example (2) has no NE or any special lexicon word associated with it. A Google search of the first part of the sentence, within the quotes, will yield 639,000 results. So we can infer it is of wordplay type. But why is it funny? The topic is human weakness, as described by Mihalcea (2006). We laugh at the manifestation of human misanthropy and the satisfaction in gloating. This relates to the relief theory of humor, as the joke is allowing us to speak about our tabooed and unsocial feelings. How can the computer understand this? It is a tricky and complex task. We could parse the sentence to find out that the reader is advised to make someones cut sting, and we could use a semantic ontology or a lexicon to teach the computer that sting is a negative experience, which will lead to drawing the correct conclusion. We believe a comprehensive understanding of the sentence is not mandatory, but if necessary, we can use the work of Taylor (2010) as reference. Example (3) ends with the short sentence true story, which tells us that this is an anecdote. The present progressive tense of the verbs implies the same. To understand this short sentence we need a semantic effort, or a lexicon of such terms that confirm the anecdotal nature of the tweet. The NE Starbucks could be set as the viable topic. Example (4) has a proper noun as NE, Tigers, recognized by its capital first letter. This is also the topic, and the type is probably vulgarity, that can be recognized by the last word in it. Example (5) is an insult, and the topic is the proper name Jay Leno. This research will likely conclude that we prefer the human NE over the nonhuman one, when instructing the computer how to choose our topic. To recognize that this is an insult to Leno, we need to know he is a comedian, and that the tweet suggests that he is not funny. An internet search will discover the former. For the latter, we must understand what translate something into funny means. The semantics of the verb and its indirect object that follows the preposition into should clarify this. This can be achieved by parsing the tweet, looking up the semantics of translate and comedian in a semantic ontology, and concluding that Leno is not funny. This is contradictory to his profession and can be viewed as an insult. Example (6) is a pun, or a wordplay, in taxonomy of Hay (1995). No topic. The pun is based on the phonologic resemblance of forth and force and the immortal quote from Star Wars. According to Wikipedia, May 4th is actually an official Star Wars day because of this pun, and an internet search can teach our computer what type of tweet this is. Alternatively, with more original phonological puns, phonologic ontologies (which have not been researched thoroughly) can be a proper reference source.

The remainder of the paper is organized as follows: related work is reviewed in section 2 . Section 3 briefly describes the data used in the experiments and evaluates the results. Section 4 describes the task and algorithm of humor classification and section5 gives ideas for further research.

2 Related Work

We will survey the research work related to our thesis in 4 different points of reference.

2.1 Humor Recognition

While the classification of different data, identifying whether tweets are humorous, sarcastic, or neither, has been examined closely in recent years, I am unaware of any research that has been done on automatic humor classification by type or topic. One of the first studies on computational humor was done by Binsted and Ritchie (1997), in which the authors modeled puns based on semantics and syntax. This work paved the way for humor generation research works, such as LIBJOG (Raskin and Attardo 1994), JAPE (Binsted and Ritchie 1994, 1997) and HAHAcronym (Stock and Strapparava, 2003). The two former systems were criticized as pseudo-generative because of the template nature of their synthesized jokes. The latter is also very limited in its syntax. Only in later studies was the recognition of humor examined. Mihalcea and Strapparava (2005) used content and stylistic features to automatically recognize humor. This was done, however, on a more homogenous set of data, one-liners, that, unlike tweets, are formal, grammatically correct and often exhibit stylistic features, such as alliteration and antonyms, which seldom appear in tweets. Davidov et al. (2010) recognized sarcastic sentences in Twitter. They used a semi-supervised algorithm to acquire features that could then be used by the classifier to decide which data item was sarcastic. In addition to these lexical patterns, the classifier also used punctuation-based features (i.e. number of !). This procedure achieved an F-score of 0.83 on the Twitter dataset and the algorithm will be carefully examined in my research.

2.2 Humor Theories

There are three theories of humor mentioned in related works: the incongruity theory, the superiority theory and the relief theory. The incongruity theory suggests that the existence of two contradictory interpretations to the same statement is a necessary condition for humor. It was used as a basis for the Semantic Script-based Theory of Humour (SSTH) (Raskin 1985), and later on the General Theory of Verbal Humour (GTVH) (Attardo and Raskin 1991). Taylor (2010) found that the semantic recognition of humor is based on this theory and on humor data that support it. We can see that examples (1)-(5) in section 1 do not comply with this theory. It appears that some humorous statements can lack any incongruity.

The superiority theory claims that humor is triggered by feelings of superiority with respect to ourselves or others from a prior event (Hobbes 1840).

The relief theory views humor as a way out of taboo and a license for banned thoughts. Through humor the energy inhibited by social etiquette can be released and bring relief to both the author and audience. Freud, as early as 1905, supported this theory and connected humor to the unconscious (Freud, 1960). Minsky (1980) embraces the theory and observes the faulty logic in humor as another steam-releasing trait. Mihalcea (2006) enumerated the most discriminative content-based features learned by her humor classifier. The more substantial features were found to be human-centric vocabulary, professional communities and human weaknesses that often appear in humorous data. We think these features of humor, more than the three theories mentioned above, will be of greatest value to our task.

2.3 Humor Types

We will then explore what research has been performed on the actual content and types of humor, aside from the computer recognition point of view. There are many taxonomies of humor (Hay, 1995), and the one that best suits our data contains the following categories:

1. Anecdotes
2. Fantasy
3. Insult
4. Irony
5. Jokes
6. Observational
7. Quote
8. Role play
9. Self deprecation

10. Vulgarity

11. Wordplay

12. Other

We believe that most of our humorous tweets will fall into one of the first 11 categories.

3 Data

Our task is to categorize the different humorous tweets. A little about Twitter: Twitter is a popular microblogging service with more than 200 million messages (tweets) sent daily. The tweet length is restricted to 140 characters. Users can subscribe to get all the tweets of a certain user, and are hence called followers of this user, but the tweets are publically available, and can be read by anyone. They may be read on the Twitter website, on many other sites, and through Twitter API, an interface that allows access to a great amount of tweets and user attributes. Aside from text, tweets often include url addresses, references to other Twitter users (appear as ¡user¿) or content tags (called hashtags and appear #¡tag¿). These tags are not taken from a set list but can be invented by the tweeter. They tend to be more generic since they are used in Twitters search engine to find tweets containing the tag. Our humorous tweet dataset is derived from websites such as `http://www.funny-tweets.com` that publish funny tweets, and can be further expanded by subscribing to all tweets by comedians who appear on these sites. Another option is a thorough check of tweets of Twitter Lists like ComedyWorld/ and features comedians who send messages to all of their followers.

3.1 Evaluation

To evaluate our results we must find out which type and topic of humor every classified tweet belongs to. We are spared from the challenging task of deciding whether a tweet is funny or not, since all of our data was already deemed funny by the publishing sites. Categorizing humor is of course very complex, due to the fuzzy nature of the taxonomy and the subjectivity of this task. One tweet can be related to more than one topic, and belong to more than one humor type. Nevertheless, the only way to achieve a gold standard for such classification is through human annotation, which can be accomplished through the use of a mechanical Turk.

4 Humor Classification

We will use a semi-supervised algorithm with a seed of labeled tweets as input. This will produce a set of distinguishing features for the multi-class classifier. A few feature types will be examined: syntactical, pattern-based, lexical, morphological, phonological and pragmatic. Here are some examples which refer to the task of classifying the examples given in section 1:

Syntactic Features

- transitiveness of the verb
- syntactic ambiguity

Pattern-based Features

- Patterns including high-frequency and content words as described in the algorithm in Davidov and Rappoport (2006)

Lexical Features

- Lexicon words like Gay
- Existence of NEs (like Facebook and Starbucks)
- Meaning of the verb and its objects(make someones cut sting)
- Lexical ambiguity

Morphological Features

- The tense of the verbs in the tweet
- Special word morphology (like the biblical eth suffix in our example (1))

Phonological Features

- existence of a word that appears on a homophones list (which could help with pun recognition)

Pragmatic Features

- Thee amount of results obtained from a search engine query of the tweet of the verbs in the tweet

Stylistic Features

- Existence of smiley characters
- Punctuation, like !

The topic of a tweet will also be retrieved from automatically retrieved features when it does not appear as a NE in the tweet.

5 Future Work

Further research could be done to classify the tweeters of the humorous tweets based on attributes of gender, age, location, etc. This could be achieved using the type and the topic of the tweets as additional features to semi-supervised classifiers. This idea was inspired by related work that found a correlation between humor and gender. In the Gender and Humor chapter of her thesis, Hay (1995) surveyed old research that claimed women are less inclined towards humor than men. Freud (1905) claimed women do not need a sense of humor because they have fewer strong taboo feelings to repress. This perception is slowly changing, with more contemporaneous work claiming that humor is different between genders. Hay concludes that:

- men are more likely to use vulgarity and quotes than women
- women are more likely to use observational humor

To a lesser degree:

- men tend to use more role play and wordplay
- women are more likely to use jocular insults

We did not find any relevant correlation studies between age, origin, and other attributes with humor, but such research has likely been explored.

References

Attardo, S., Raskin, V. 1991. *Script theory revisited: Joke similarity and joke repre- sentation model. Humor: International Journal of Humor Research 4*, 3-4.

Cheng, Z., Caverlee, J., Lee, K. 2010. *You Are Where You Tweet: A Content-Based Approach to Geolocating Twitter Usersl.* Proceeding of the ACL conference 2010

Davidov, D., and Tsur, O. 2010. *Semi-Supervised Recognition of Sarcastic Sentences in Twitter and Amazon* Computational Linguistics, July, 107-116.

Freud, S. 1905. *Der Witz und seine Beziehung zum Unbewussten*

Freud, S. 1960. *Jokes and their relation to the unconscious* International Journal of Psychoanalysis 9

Hay, J. 1995. *Gender and Humour: Beyond a Joke.* Master thesis.

Hobbes, T. 1840. *Human Nature in English Works.* Molesworth.

Mihalcea, R. 2006. *Learning to laugh automatically: Computational models for humor recognition.* Computational Intelligence, 222.

Mihalcea, R. and Strapparava, C. 2005. *Making Computers Laugh: Investigations in Automatic Humor Recognition.* roceedings of the Conference on Human Language Technology and Empirical Methods in Natural Language Processing

Minsky, M. 1980. *Jokes and the logic of the cognitive unconscious.* Tech. rep., MIT Artificial Intelligence Laboratory.

Pennacchiotti, M. and Popescu, A. 2011. *Democrats , Republicans and Starbucks Afficionados: User Classification in Twitter.* Statistics, 430-438.

Rao, D., Yarowsky, D., Shreevats, A. and Gupta, M. 2010. *Classifying Latent User Attributes in Twitter.* Science, 37-44.

Raskin, V. 1985. *Semantic Mechanisms of Humor.* Kluwer Academic Publications

Solomon, R. 2002. *Ethics and Values in the Information Age.* Wadsworth.

Taylor, J. M. 2010. *Ontology-based view of natural language meaning: the case of humor detection.* Journal of Ambient Intelligence and Humanized Computing, 13, 221-234.

Ziv A. 1988. *National Styles of Humor.* Greenwood Press, Inc.

Author Index